how to be you

how to be you

say goodbye to should, would and could so that **you can**

Ellie Middleton

PENGUIN LIFE

AN IMPRINT OF

PENGUIN BOOKS

PENGUIN LIFE

UK | USA | Canada | Ireland | Australia
India | New Zealand | South Africa

Penguin Life is part of the Penguin Random House group of companies
whose addresses can be found at global.penguinrandomhouse.com.

Penguin
Random House
UK

First published 2024
002

Copyright © Ellie Middleton, 2024

The moral right of the author has been asserted

Set in 10/16pt Proxima Nova
Typeset by Jouve (UK), Milton Keynes
Printed and bound in Great Britain by Clays Ltd, Elcograf S.p.A.

The authorized representative in the EEA is Penguin Random House Ireland,
Morrison Chambers, 32 Nassau Street, Dublin D02 YH68

A CIP catalogue record for this book is available from the British Library

ISBN: 978-0-241-71037-1

www.greenpenguin.co.uk

MIX
Paper | Supporting
responsible forestry
FSC® C018179

Penguin Random House is committed to a
sustainable future for our business, our readers
and our planet. This book is made from Forest
Stewardship Council® certified paper.

To Mum, Dad & Lewis

People joke about having to settle for buying their parents a candle or a box of chocolates for their birthday when they deserve the whole world, and I've somehow ended up publishing my first book on Mum's birthday and my second book on Dad's. I'm sorry for stealing the limelight (again!), and I hope you know that these achievements are just as much yours as they are mine. Thank you for always supporting me to become who I am in a world that hasn't always been the kindest. x

Contents

Introduction

To be completely honest with you, working out where to start with writing this book got me **all tangled up**. When I first spoke with my lovely editor, Amy, about the possibility of creating an actionable follow-up to my first book, **unmasked**, the ADHD novelty hit (which I'm sure so many of you can relate to when starting a new project) kicked in. I felt excited, full of ideas, and eager to share all the many techniques of figuring out how to work **with** your busy brain rather than against it that I've picked up along the way with the world.

In the foreword that I wrote for my wonderful friend Leanne's book **ADHD An A to Z**, I shared that 'Learning how to hack your ADHD – and how to work with your brain rather than against it – is absolutely life-changing. But none of it is rocket science. It's a series of tiny changes, minute switches and small habits that all add together to make a huge amount of difference to your life.' Writing this follow-up guide was going to be my chance to pull all those things into one actionable resource . . . This would be super exciting, right?

Right???????

Well, it started out that way. On an initial call discussing the idea with my editor, I reeled off a whole array of possible tasks, worksheets, learnings and techniques which the book could include. My busy brain was whirring in the way it does best; I was oozing the creativity and enthusiasm which remain my very favourite parts of my interest-led, neurodivergent busy brain.

Then (and I'm sure this will be a **very** familiar experience for so many of you reading this book), I jumped off the call and did . . .

Nothing.

As a novelty-seeking ADHDer who professes to know *quite* a bit about her brain, I should probably recognize by now that if I'm not jumping headfirst into a new and exciting project, it's usually a sign that **something is not quite right**. But I pushed the thought away, smiled along, and told my friends just how thrilled I was to be cooking up a new book idea . . . While doing absolutely **nothing** about it behind the scenes.

It took until my next ADHD coaching session, a week later, when I mentioned that I'd been procrastinating about getting started, for me to identify what was really going on. After starting the coaching session by brain-dumping some of the ideas that I'd already shared with my editor, I quickly felt that familiar panicked and agitated feeling rising in my chest. I felt overwhelmed and stressed, and, to be completely honest with you, I had to hold back tears. When my coach asked me exactly what it was about starting this ever-so-exciting project that felt so stressful, I said that it was . . . the **whole thing**.

First, the fact that, as an autistic ADHDer, there are two **constantly** opposing sides of my brain that **consistently** demand **entirely different things** from me.

One loves structure and routine; one can't stick to a schedule for the life of her.

One thrives on repeated patterns; one needs novelty to stay interested.

One needs to take things one step at a time; one wants to be doing a hundred different tasks all at once.

One needs to prioritize rest; one needs to be stimulated at all times.

If I, myself, have so many opposing and clashing needs, how could I possibly pull all of those together to create a journal or workbook that was useful to both sides of my *own* brain – let alone useful to anybody else?

How could I keep it exciting and novel enough for my ADHD brain, while keeping it structured enough for my autistic brain, too?

Second, and leading on from this, I felt overwhelmed because trying to work out how to structure this guide confronted one **really big thing** that felt **really tricky** for me to admit (and that came with a big old side order of the dreaded *shame* we all know so well):

I haven't ever figured any of this out myself.

Let me be clear: I absolutely, categorically, do **not** have my shit together . . . By **any** stretch of the imagination.

Some days I'm frantically running around ticking a million things off my to-do list; some days I'm procrastinating until the very last minute.

Some days I'm too overwhelmed to even get out of bed; some days I'm chronically burned out.

Some days I achieve a million things in record time; some days I achieve nothing at all.

The reason I don't have a journal or a method or a definitive answer as to how to work with a busy brain already is that I've never found one that works — or, even if I **have** for a short stretch of time, I've inevitably fallen off the horse a week or so later. I have a drawer full of desk planners and journals that I've been convinced will be the secret to **finally** getting me organized once and for all, but that now lie unused with only a page or two ever written on. I have a home screen full of apps that promised to be the answer to all my problems, most of which were used for a fortnight at best. Over the last two years, I've shared hundreds of tips, tricks, routines and techniques for learning how to work with your neurodivergent brain rather than against it, but, in reality, I've **never actually figured it out myself**.

This is quite an uncomfortable thing to admit — especially when, as someone who grew up undiagnosed, you tend to think of yourself as a 'fully capable and functional' human being and, no matter how hard you try to accept your struggles, you are still full to the brim with a whole load of internalized ableism. It's difficult to be confronted with the fact that actually, being an autistic ADHDer is pretty damn disabling, and that each and every day it can feel like a slog to get even the simplest things done, or to end the day without feeling absolutely frazzled.

However, after a little step back, a few deep breaths, and a couple of conversations with the people I trust the most, I came up with a solution. I realized that I just **did not** have the answer to a one-size-fits-all, fail-proof, definitive method of how to 'handle life' as an autistic ADHDer – so there was no use desperately trying to dig one up from somewhere. Even if I **did** find a life-management strategy that felt like it ticked all the right boxes and was The Answer, it was likely that the novelty would wear off soon enough when I tried to implement it myself – and that that would also be the case for so many of the busy brains that the book was designed to support in the first place.

Rather than focusing on what I thought I 'should' do, I needed to take a piece of my own advice and, instead, focus on doing what felt **best for my brain** (and what would, therefore, suit the brains of the other autistic ADHDers who might come to this book for support, too). Rather than prescribing 'The Ellie Middleton Method for Life' (which, quite frankly, was non-existent), I could instead share a whole range of tips, tricks and things to consider when working with a neurodivergent brain, which each reader could pick and choose from to find the combination which best worked for them. Then, whenever the time might come when they inevitably found themselves veering off from the method of choice, they could come back, flick through, and pick a new one.

So, that's what we have here:

A whole bunch of tips, some of which you might find useful, and some of which you might not.

You won't be able to implement them all at the same time, but there are enough different ones to (hopefully) keep you engaged, productive and feeling good for a pretty decent period of time. The most important thing is that you approach the task of learning to work with your brain with **curiosity**; remember that it is a challenge to be solved, a problem to be calculated, and an experiment to be engaged in. There is no magic wand solution, and there is no one-size-fits-all approach. But, with trial and error, you **will** find ways of working, living and being that better suit your brain.

Another important thing that I'd like you to know (in case it wasn't clear from the minor breakdown I've just described that occurred when I was faced with this task) is this:

I get it.

You might have come to terms with having the neurodivergent brain that you do, and you might feel committed to being your true, unmasked self, but even if that is the case — which I'm aware it isn't for many — it is still **incredibly** tricky sometimes. However much you're proud of who you are, and however much you're thankful for finally getting some answers about how your brain works, living with a neurodivergent brain in a neurotypical world can be tough. As I shared in ***unmasked***:

When you are diagnosed with a neurodivergent condition, whether that's by a medical professional or by researching and self-diagnosing, there is no 'handbook' on what to do next. There are no guides, often no therapy, and often no support to turn to. After a medical diagnostic assessment, it's usually a case of hearing the words, 'Yes, you do, in fact, have xxx,' and then leaving your assessment with little more than a cheery wave goodbye, a bucketful of questions and a mountain of unresolved trauma.

There is a real lack of easy-to-digest, accessible or actionable resources out there for you to learn from, but hopefully, this book will be the first step in changing that.

Some of these tips might seem pretty simple – but sometimes, it's the tiniest changes that can make the biggest difference! I often say that my brain is like a toddler, and I have to trick it into doing what I want it to. If I give my toddler brain a little bit of what it wants, it will, hopefully, give me a little bit of what I want in return. If my brain wants to be a stubborn toddler, I will happily be an even more stubborn parent – and if that means playing games, role-playing, or giving out sweeties as rewards, then so be it!

It's also incredibly important to remember that a lot of the things that we shame ourselves for, and standards that we get hung up on, are actually just a big old pile of **rubbish**. We live in a Western society that is incredibly neuronormative, meaning that we tend to take neurotypical ways of being, working and functioning as 'the norm' and think that every other way is 'wrong' or 'bad'. That simply is not the case, but these neuronormative standards can trick us into believing it to be true, and therefore shaming ourselves, holding ourselves to unrealistic standards, or doing things a certain way because we feel like we 'should' rather than for any actual useful reason. We'll dig into this a little bit more before we get into the chapters themselves, as it's something very important to have in mind, but I wanted to make it clear right from the get-go that this isn't going to be a book of hacks of 'how to appear to be neurotypical when you're actually neurodivergent' or 'how to GirlBoss your way out of ADHD', because that is **never** going to be something that I advocate for.

I really hope that, over the following pages, you'll find some tips and tricks which will help you to work with your busy brain rather than against it, and to Get Stuff Done while being a happy and healthy human. I also hope that you will feel reminded that there is **no moral value to productivity** and that you're allowed to be a human **being** sometimes, instead of always feeling like a human **doing**. I really want this to be a book that helps you find ways of navigating the world more easily but, more importantly, of doing it in a way that suits **you**. I hope that, throughout the book, you'll find tips and tricks that will help you to be a fuller, truer version of yourself – so you can be **YOU**.

Good luck – take it slow and steady, and remember that we're all doing this together. A big part of figuring out your neurodivergence is simply learning to work with your brain rather than against it, and letting go of all the 'shoulds' we've been told about how we 'should' behave, 'should' function, 'should' do things and 'should' feel. One of my very favourite paragraphs from **unmasked**, which I think is just as important to remember while reading this book, is the following:

If you can learn how to work with your brain rather than against it, discover who you really are under the mask that you have learned to carry throughout your whole life, and work towards accepting and maybe even loving the real you, it really is possible to find a happiness that has always felt just out of reach. I say this because I know it's true – I never thought that the level of joy, acceptance for myself and success (whatever that means) that I experience today was something that would ever be available to me, and yet here I am.

See you on the other side!

However much you're proud of who you are, and however much you're thankful for finally getting some answers about how your brain works, living with a neurodivergent brain in a neurotypical world can be tough.

A big part of figuring out your neurodivergence is simply learning to work with your brain rather than against it, and letting go of all the 'shoulds' we've been told about how we 'should' behave, 'should' function, 'should' do things and 'should' feel.

How to use this book and what to expect

Before we get started, I think it's important to remind you that this book is designed to help **support you** and make your life easier – **not** to make it trickier or shame you into feeling inadequate. Although I'll be sharing tips which will (hopefully) help teach you how to work with your brain rather than against it, that doesn't mean that I'm expecting you to finish reading this book, magically adopt every single tool, skill and strategy, and suddenly become an über-organized #GirlBoss productivity queen. This book is not designed to teach you how to mask, how to make the struggles associated with your neurodivergence 'disappear', or how to 'function' like a neurotypical person; it's designed to help you find strategies for working with your brain to do the things that matter, and to let go of the things that don't.

With that said, I want you to remove **any** pressure you might be putting on yourself to read this book all in one go, or in the 'right' order, or to immediately adopt and implement every single tip as you read it.

If you've read my first book, *unmasked*, you might recognize the way that we've structured this second book, too:

- **Each chapter can stand alone, so if you're just looking for a particular something right now, you can jump straight to it, and it will still all make sense.**

- Everything will be bite-sized and digestible, written by a whizzy brain, for whizzy brains.

- There is absolutely no pressure whatsoever to read this book in any specific way; what matters is that you use it as a tool to support **you**. So if you want to read the whole thing from start to finish? That's fine! If you want to focus on one chapter at a time? Go ahead. If it all feels a little bit overwhelming and you want to read one tip, close the book, and not come back until that habit is formed? That's perfectly okay.

In short, this book is designed to help you work through any overwhelm, not to add to it — so please know that it is okay to take your time and use it in whichever way feels most helpful for you.

We've also recorded *how to be you* as an audiobook, so you have the option of listening along while you're reading if you feel as though that might help. If you do choose to listen, I highly recommend cranking the speed up to 1.5x or 2x, as this can help interest-led ADHD brains concentrate.

Now that we've got those expectations out of the way, I think it makes sense to start by explaining how I've chosen to structure this book and why I thought that might be helpful. As I've already mentioned, my aim with this guide is to share a whole range of tips, tricks and things to consider when working with a neurodivergent brain. You won't be able to implement them all at once; however, you can flick through, take the bits that feel like they might be useful, discard the bits that don't, and come back and add more to your repertoire as and when you feel it might be helpful. It's essentially a pick and mix of 'things to consider which might make your life a bit easier', or maybe even something a bit more like Blockbuster – you can borrow the tip (or DVD) while it helps you, and then bring it back a short while later to exchange it for another.

I've decided to structure the tips, tricks and strategies around the **eight executive functioning skills** that we all have. This is because a considerable part of ADHD, autism, and many other neurodivergences is a difference (not deficit!) in these executive functioning skills.

Executive functioning skills, as described by Harvard University, are 'the mental processes that enable us to plan, focus attention, remember instructions, and juggle multiple tasks successfully'. In the same way that an air traffic control system at a busy airport safely manages the arrival and departure of many aircraft across multiple runways, the brain needs our executive functions to filter distractions, prioritize tasks, set and achieve goals, and control our impulses. The eight executive functions are:

1. **Working memory** – the ability to hold and manipulate information for short-term use.

2. **Self-monitoring** – the ability to observe and evaluate your own thoughts, behaviours, and actions.

3. **Inhibition/impulse control** – the ability to resist impulsive urges and hold back from inappropriate or disruptive behaviours.

4. **Emotional regulation** – the ability to recognize, understand and effectively manage your emotions and reactions to different situations.

5. **Flexibility** – the ability to adapt and adjust to changing circumstances, perspectives or demands.

6. **Planning and prioritization** – the ability to create a systematic approach to achieving goals, including breaking tasks into steps and determining their relative importance.

7. **Task initiation** – the ability to independently begin a task or activity without procrastination or hesitation.

8. **Organization** – the ability to structure and arrange information, materials or physical spaces.

As you may already know, the word **neurodivergent**, first coined by Kassiane Asasumasu in 2000, is an umbrella term which includes innate and genetic conditions (including ADHD and autism) as well as acquired or developed conditions. Since anyone who **functions in a way that diverges from dominant societal norms, standards and expectations** falls under the neurodivergent umbrella, it makes sense that our executive functions would be a big part of what causes us to diverge, and, therefore, informs our identity of being neurodivergent. If the way that you think, learn, behave, communicate, process information or feel emotions diverges from societal norms, you are neurodivergent, and our executive functioning skills play a big part in what causes us to think, learn, behave, communicate, process information and feel emotions in those divergent ways.

It's also important to point out here that this definition of neurodivergent – anyone who thinks, learns, behaves, communicates, processes information or feels emotions differently from societal norms – is the one that stands true throughout this book. Although I will often talk about ADHD and autism (because that is the frame of reference that I have personally), when I say neurodivergent I don't just mean 'autistic people' or 'ADHDers'. If you have come to this book because the normal ways of working and being don't work for you, then the label of neurodivergent is yours to claim. If you think, learn, behave, communicate, process information or feel emotions differently from most people, then you are neurodivergent – regardless of whether you have a specific diagnosis or not.

Executive functioning skills are impacted in people with many different neurodivergences. Studies indicate that people with ADHD have approximately a 30% delay in the development of their executive functions, and that adults with ADHD tend to only develop approximately 75–80% of the executive functioning capability of their peers (which are usually fully developed by the age of thirty). Additionally, according to the NHS, 'some research suggests that up to 80% of those with autism suffer from executive function disorder, leading to difficulties managing time, completing tasks, and making what might be thought of as simple tasks – like cleaning your room – very complicated or seemingly impossible'. The use of the word 'disorder' here feels a little icky to me; however, the sentiment stands that ADHDers, autistic people, and a whole range of other neurodivergent folks can find Getting Stuff Done exceptionally difficult.

For each of the eight executive functions (and therefore the eight main chapters of the book), I have:

- **Started out with a clear and simple introduction that will tell you what to expect over the following pages.**

- Shared two key quotes for you to remember (feel free to rip these out and stick them somewhere in plain sight, or snap a picture to keep as your phone wallpaper!).

- Followed this with a longer section, digging deeper into what that executive function is, the ways it might impact our lives, the things that might make it tricky for neurodivergent people, and the structures and systems that have informed or impacted the ways we think about that executive function in our society.

- I've then shared a quick-fire list of accommodations, reasonable adjustments or 'things to ask for' which might help to support neurodivergent brains.

- After the quick-fire list, there are five more in-depth strategies, tools, worksheets or methods which you might want to consider, to equip you to work with your brain rather than against it. (As a reminder, you won't be able to – and aren't expected to attempt to! – implement all these tips at the same time; they are there as more of a pick-and-mix for you to choose the strategies that might feel helpful and leave the others behind for another time.)

- Finally, I've condensed the chapter down into a little recap section and shared some final takeaways for you to consider.

Hopefully, this structure will feel bite-sized and actionable and leave you walking away with lots of things to consider and think about – without feeling overwhelmed or pressured in any way to implement the changes into your life.

As well as making you think about the ways that you support and accommodate your own brain, I hope you will walk away questioning how our society currently functions. Perhaps, like me, you will also realize that many of the neuronormative systems and rules that we feel pressured to follow aren't actually effective, or helpful, or necessary to carry forward. Hopefully, you will be able to let go of any shame that you might have felt in the past about the way that you have (or haven't) been able to 'function', think, learn, behave and process, and finally be more *you*.

What defines our view of executive functioning?

In the Introduction, I briefly touched on the shame that we might have been made to feel for the way that our brains work. To follow on from this, I think it's essential that, before getting into any of the specific executive functioning skills or arming ourselves with ways to better accommodate our brains, we take some time to set the scene regarding the history and culture that have led us to think of executive functions in the way that we do. Many of the ways that our executive functioning skills are framed, and many of the standards we get hung up on, and therefore things that we might shame ourselves for, are (for want of a better word) **a made-up pile of rubbish**. The 'right way' of doing things, or of *being*, is a social construct defined by the systems and biases that inform almost every aspect of our society, including:

- White supremacy

- Patriarchy

- Capitalism

- Colonialism

- Ableism

These systems of oppression, I'm sure you will agree, are each **incredibly** meaty, complicated and nuanced topics, which individually would require **multiple** books to properly do them justice. I obviously do not have the space to do that here, and I am also very aware of the fact that as a White, British, cisgender, economically privileged woman, I am probably not the best person to speak on each of these systems of oppression – as many of them I will have benefited from hugely throughout the course of my life.

However, I believe that in order to unlearn the 'shoulds' that society has enforced on us our entire lives, to allow ourselves to have the space to do things differently, and to let go of shame, we **must** have a basic understanding of each of these systems of oppression. The following pages should start to give you a fundamental understanding of these, which will be helpful to bear in mind while we explore the eight executive functioning skills throughout the rest of the book. However, I urge you to go on to do further reading, listening, learning and questioning about each of these subjects, and especially to listen to those whose intersecting identities of race, gender, sexuality and disability mean that they are marginalized by multiple systems of oppression.

In this chapter, we will explore:

- **Which systems of oppression have impacted the way we think about executive functioning?**

- **How do these systems define what is considered 'normal' vs 'disordered'?**

- **What can we do to begin to resist these systems of oppression and exist in a way that feels true to us?**

To begin to let go of shame, we must have a basic understanding of the systems of oppression that inform the hierarchy, rules, expectations and demands of Western society.

We fear not being good enough, not feeling accepted, not belonging, and not doing things right.

White supremacy

White supremacy, as defined by Layla F. Saad in her incredibly powerful book *Me and White Supremacy: How to Recognise Your Privilege, Combat Racism and Change the World*, is 'a racist ideology based upon the belief that White people are superior in many ways to people of other races and that, therefore, White people should be dominant over other races'. Saad (who, since writing *Me and White Supremacy*, has discovered her own neurodivergence later in life) goes on to explain that 'White supremacy is not just an attitude or way of thinking. It also extends to how systems and institutions are structured to uphold this White dominance.' Many people incorrectly believe that White supremacy is a belief only held by far-right extremists, but, in reality, it is a racist and harmful undercurrent that runs through **all** White-centred or Western societies and, therefore, informs our norms, rules and laws.

In 1999, Tema Okun published an article called **'White Supremacy Culture'**, which listed fifteen characteristics that she and her late colleague Kenneth Jones believed define and shape our society. This article has since been updated and expanded, and the characteristics that Okun outlines explain the way that these White supremacy characteristics impact the way that humans are behaving, living and functioning in Western society. As I'm sure you will see, these ways of behaving and functioning are very closely related to our earlier list of executive functioning skills and, therefore, have a huge impact on what we consider to be 'normal'. Below is a list of some of the key characteristics that affect our overarching relationship with what we deem to be 'normal' executive functioning vs executive 'dysfunction', and you will also meet some more of Okun's characteristics throughout the rest of the book, as we dig a little more deeply into each of the executive functions.

As you read through the characteristics, it might be helpful to reflect (or make notes) on the ways that these characteristics show up for you, or the times that you have experienced them in action in other people's behaviour. It is really important that we identify the ways that White supremacy affects our society, and to remember that you are not alone and that we are all impacted by these ways of being. When we begin to identify the biases that have shaped our society, or the 'shoulds' that have been imposed upon us, we can let go of them and find ways of working, functioning and behaving that work better for each of us, both as individuals and as a collective.

1. Fear

In White supremacy culture, we are made to feel afraid. We fear not being good enough, not feeling accepted, not belonging, and not doing things right. This characteristic is an undercurrent throughout all of the other characteristics and informs the way that we behave and make decisions because we are always desperately trying to avoid the 'bad' thing that would be the result of not doing as we're supposed to – whether that is perceived failure, ostracization or any other consequence.

How fear influences how we feel we 'should' behave:

— We often feel that we must behave, work, or function in the ways deemed 'normal' or we will be criticized or ostracized.

— Our society imposes a constant fear of failure or of not being good enough, which might lead us to assign moral value to the ways that we function (e.g. our productivity levels), putting more pressure on us to work in a certain way.

— We fear the consequences of not being able to function or 'do things' in the way that other people can, and so often work incredibly hard behind the scenes to keep up appearances.

2. Perfectionism

Perfectionism is the belief that things can be done perfectly, or that people can be (and should aim to be) 'perfect', based on a socially constructed standard. This constant striving for perfection reinforces White supremacy culture because, while we are focused on working towards 'perfection' (whatever 'perfect' means), our energy and attention are being used up, and so we might never get the chance to stop and ask ourselves **why** we're working so hard towards this so-called perfection (which is most likely just to keep perpetuating our White supremacy, capitalist culture) — i.e. to realize that this benefits the White supremacy culture that we are all living in. Perfection is also something that is seen as a **fixed point** to strive towards or a destination to arrive at (although we never quite seem to get there), rather than recognizing that this endless pursuit is pointless, as we are all born perfect.

How perfectionism influences how we feel we 'should' behave:

— An emphasis on perfectionism means that we're always striving to be more productive or achieve more things, rather than accepting that we're fine just the way we are and instead questioning the systems in place.

— As a society, we constantly push ourselves to our limits to 'improve' or 'grow', even when it doesn't suit us, which means that we assign a disproportionate amount of significance to our executive functioning capabilities like organization or prioritization.

— It encourages us to see things in a very black-and-white way, which means that we might think that if we are not 'perfect', then we have outright failed — rather than acknowledging that there is no such thing as perfect and that 'good' is good enough.

3. One Right Way

Linked to perfectionism, One Right Way is the belief that there is one correct way to do something, and any divergence or difference from that way is seen to be 'bad' or 'wrong'. Okun compares this to how a missionary might arrive in a new culture and only see value in their own beliefs, and try to 'convert' the people they meet to these personal beliefs, rather than acknowledging any value in the culture that is different from their own.

For me, this reminded me of how, in maths exams at school, you were given marks for the 'working out' that led you to your answer – and if you hadn't used the techniques that had been taught in the curriculum, you could lose marks **even** when getting to the correct answer. As someone whose brain has often diverged from the 'right' way of doing things and who doesn't value social constructs in the same way that most people might, I have definitely felt the effects of One Right Way!

How One Right Way influences how we feel we 'should' behave:

    – One Right Way causes us to think that we have to do things 'the way they have always been done', even if that way doesn't suit our brains. This forces us to work against our brain's natural ways of thinking, functioning and processing.

    – We are held to neuronormative ways of living and doing things rather than appreciating that everyone has different ways of working, behaving, thinking and being.

    – Society often tells us that we 'just have to get on with it', and frequently deters us from questioning the established ways of doing things.

4. Paternalism

Paternalism tells us that certain people (often of a specific age, gender and race, namely older, White men) are the ones who hold power and, therefore, get to define what is 'perfect' or 'the right way'. They also get to make decisions on behalf of the people who don't hold the same power they do and might not think that it is important or necessary to consider other people's thoughts, beliefs, viewpoints or experiences. Think of when you would ask your parents something as a child, and their answer would be, 'Because I said so!' Paternalism feels very apparent in the UK Government at the time of writing (Winter 2023), as a small number of people in the Tory leadership continue to make decisions in Parliament regarding foreign affairs, immigration, benefits, transport, social support and many other things, which don't seem to, in any way, reflect the needs, beliefs or wants of the majority of the population which the Government was designed to serve. Paternalism means that those without power are kept in the dark about decision-making processes, even when they are the people who will most feel the impact of those decisions.

How paternalism influences how we feel we 'should' behave:

– As I explored in *unmasked*, the diagnostic criteria for many neurodivergences, including both autism and ADHD, are based on research done on almost exclusively young, White, cis boys.

– This research, including the ways we define what is 'functional' and 'dysfunctional', was completed by a very small number of psychiatrists (most of whom were also middle-class, White, educated men), and is seen as definitive and final rather than just one opinion.

– Psychiatrists and medical professionals (who are often neurotypical) often hold all the power in defining what is 'normal' vs what is 'disordered', and what the 'treatment' or 'solution' for the 'disordered' behaviour should be, rather than that power being in the hands of the person themselves. In extreme cases, this can lead to many autistic people, for example, being institutionalized against their will for not being able to behave in the ways that have been categorized as 'normal'.

5. Either/Or and the binary

Either/Or thinking defines the way that many things in our society are seen in a very black-and-white way – we see something as either good **OR** bad, or right **OR** wrong. In reality, the vast majority of things, people, decisions and options in life are incredibly nuanced and a combination of both good **AND** bad, or right **AND** wrong. Either/Or thinking causes us to simplify issues which are actually very complicated and nuanced, like assuming that someone who steals is always and categorically a '**bad**' person – when in reality, they might be stealing in order to feed their family and be unemployed due to being marginalized by multiple systems of oppression.

How Either/Or influences how we feel we 'should' behave:

— Since things are seen as good **OR** bad, or right **OR** wrong, any divergence from 'normal' ways of functioning is seen as inherently bad/wrong.

— Support needs or differences are seen in a very either/or way: people are considered to be either 'normal' or 'having executive dysfunction', with no in-between, which neglects the nuanced and complex nature of spiky profiles (more on this in my first book, *unmasked*) and how our needs and differences might change day-to-day or over the course of time.

— This means that those who are higher masking or have generally lower support needs might not be able to access support. The binary way of thinking encourages us to see people as either 'completely fine' or 'unable to do anything'; if you aren't seen to be struggling 'enough' to qualify for 'unable to do anything', then you, therefore, are seen as being 'completely fine' and require no support.

6. Defensiveness

In White supremacy culture, defensiveness explains the way that we might not be open to any questioning, criticism or curiosity, and that we might value protecting the status quo (or a person's best interests) instead of searching for the truth or best outcome. For example, if somebody raises concerns in a company about racial microaggressions, a leader might jump to defending themselves and denying that they are racist, rather than actually looking into the claims or trying to resolve them. This characteristic means that things are often stuck 'the way they have always been done' rather than people or organizations being open to change or new ways of thinking.

How defensiveness influences how we feel we 'should' behave:

– In a defensive society, we see any form of questioning as a threat, rather than valuing curiosity and challenging the status quo as an effective way to find better outcomes. This means that we are forced to stick to the way that things have always been done, which might mean functioning and working in ways that aren't necessarily best suited for our brains, rather than being able to challenge and question these norms in search of positive change.

– When we get stuck in defensive ways of thinking, individuals might be less open to finding new, better and more inclusive ways of working.

– We see any divergence from the norm as a bad thing, and so people might not want to acknowledge their differences or struggles and, therefore, not access support or explore their own neurodivergence.

7. Denial

Denial is an extension of defensiveness, which describes the way that people or organizations will jump to denying any accusations of wrongdoing rather than taking the time to explore or consider the claims. They might refuse to consider or acknowledge history or say outright that genuine claims are simply not true.

How denial influences how we feel we 'should' behave:

– Companies or employers might deny that current ways of working are unhelpful or damaging for those of us whose brains function differently, and so be reluctant to make any changes. The same could even occur within families, where parents are in denial that the ways **they** were parented had room for improvement, and so carry on the same unhelpful or damaging patterns with their children.

– Often, challenges themselves are actually denied outright, with people thinking that people are 'making them up' or just 'not trying hard enough'.

– People might deny or refuse to believe that the way we have historically pathologized any deviation from the 'normal' ways of behaving, thinking, functioning or being has been harmful to women and people marginalized for their gender, people of colour, and disabled and neurodivergent people. This means that marginalized people continue to be labelled, pathologized, ostracized, institutionalized and even incarcerated simply for being different, rather than us as a society understanding that difference is simply part of human nature.

8. Right to comfort

This characteristic explains the way that in Western culture, individuals often feel as though they have a right to feel comfortable – whether that is emotional comfort or psychological comfort. One major example we see of this is in the way that when horrific atrocities are happening across the world, many people choose to disengage from the news or social media narrative because watching or hearing about the events taking place makes us feel uncomfortable or uneasy. While this is very nuanced, and we all need to protect our mental health to some degree, being able to disengage at all is a huge privilege, and we should learn to question whether our right to comfort takes precedence over our responsibility to do the right thing.

How right to comfort influences how we feel we 'should' behave:

– In a world where those in power are led to believe that their comfort is a right, they are less inclined to accommodate others in a way which might affect that level of comfort by demanding energy, or different ways of working, from them. For example, in a typical office setting they might refuse to share written rather than verbal instructions, as they feel this adds more to their workload.

– Prioritizing comfort might lead some individuals (e.g. those who are benefiting from current ways of working) to resist changes or adaptations necessary to accommodate those who struggle with executive functioning.

– The idea that we have a 'right to comfort' can contribute to a reluctance to address systemic issues which neurodivergent people, or those who do things differently, might face. Instead of recognizing and addressing structural barriers, individuals are likely to prioritize their personal comfort, and therefore overlook the need for systemic changes in education, workplaces or social environments.

9. Power hoarding

As the name suggests, a key part of White supremacy culture is that the vast majority of the power is held by a small group of people, and there is no real interest from that group in sharing any of their power. Power is seen as a finite resource, with only so much to go around. This can lead to those who **do** hold power feeling threatened when anyone suggests changes in how things should be done. We can see this hierarchy and structure throughout society; for example, a CEO being reluctant to share power within their business, or a father wanting to maintain power in a patriarchal family unit.

How power hoarding influences how we feel we 'should' behave:

– In workplaces, an autistic person questioning why something is done a certain way or why something has been asked of them in an attempt to gain clarity and understanding might (incorrectly) be accused of questioning authority, and, therefore, be viewed as a threat or a disruptor, and face challenges as a result.

– The 'power' of deciding what is deemed 'normal' vs 'disordered' typically lies with psychiatrists or other health professionals, rather than each individual being able to define what is normal for them.

– Those with power in organizations or workplaces might assume that those wanting change (i.e. to be accommodated for their executive functioning differences, or to implement new, more inclusive policies) are ill-informed, emotional or inexperienced, rather than considering that they could be right.

As I'm sure you will have noticed while reading through these White supremacy characteristics, many of them match up very closely with the ways we have been told are the 'right' way to do things, and therefore define what is considered 'normal' executive functioning vs executive 'dysfunction'. As Sonny Jane Wise (they/them) explains in their book *We're All Neurodiverse*: 'We need to recognize executive functioning as a set of neuronormative standards and expectations that are unrealistic for many individuals. I don't believe we can do that without unpacking, deconstructing and challenging White supremacy culture.'

You will see more of Tema Okun's characteristics of White supremacy throughout the book as we dig further into each individual executive functioning skill, and I would also strongly recommend that you do further reading on White supremacy in order to better understand the way that it shapes our society. The following resources are a fantastic starting point:

- *Me and White Supremacy: How to Recognise Your Privilege, Combat Racism and Change the World* by Layla F. Saad.

- *Why I'm No Longer Talking to White People about Race* by Reni Eddo-Lodge.

- *Dismantling Racism: A Workbook for Social Change Groups* by Kenneth Jones and Tema Okun.

Patriarchy

Another system of oppression that defines the way we all think about executive functioning is patriarchy. **Patriarchy**, as defined by Professor Sylvia Walby OBE, Professor of Criminology at Royal Holloway University of London, is a 'system of social structures and practices in which men dominate, oppress, and exploit women'. It is a social system predominantly defined by men, in which men hold a privileged position. Much of Western society is defined by patriarchy: in the UK alone, women carry out around 60% more unpaid work than men, spending more time on cooking, cleaning and childcare.

In *unmasked*, I wrote a chapter called **'The Lost Generation'**, in which I explained the ways that our patriarchal systems have a huge impact on the number of women and people marginalized for their gender who remain undiagnosed, misdiagnosed or late-diagnosed for autism, ADHD and other neurodevelopmental conditions and neurodivergences. Research has suggested that 80% of autistic women remain undiagnosed at the age of eighteen, while another study found that boys were diagnosed with autism at an average age of four years.

This is thought to be down to the fact that the research initially undertaken into autism (as well as ADHD and other neurodivergences) was majoritively based on studies of **young, White, cis boys**. Kanner, one of the earliest researchers into autism, studied **eight boys and three girls**, while two other early researchers, Asperger and Sukhareva, worked with **all male samples**. Hans Asperger even stated that he had 'never met a girl with the fully-fledged picture of autism'. This meant that the research that followed also mostly had all-male samples because the stereotype had been created that girls (or women and people marginalized for their gender) just 'weren't autistic'.

This being said, our lack of access to a timely and accurate diagnosis of autism, ADHD and other neurodivergences isn't the only way we, as neurodivergent people and those who have differences in their executive functioning skills, are impacted by patriarchy. As **Gina Martin** (she/her), campaigner, speaker and author of *No Offence, But . . .: How to Have Difficult Conversations for Meaningful Change,* explains:

> As bell hooks names it: 'imperialist white supremacist capitalist patriarchy' is the social system built by cis elite men. They built systems, institutions and processes for themselves, excluding people who weren't men and who experienced any kind of

neurodivergence or disability. So, it's not at all surprising that neurodivergent folks, especially marginalized ones, build out their own constellations of tricks, mechanisms, and systems to navigate what these men built.

From homes and domestic expectations, to exam halls and the education system, what was created was ultimately to form a labour class which upheld optimization, self-ascension and elite capitalism. When it comes to ADHD, we know girls are diagnosed much less or later than boys, in part because of society's biases and assumptions about emotions and how we heavily gender them. Girls are socialized to be agreeable, small and facilitating – which is a masking of its own kind – and that plays heavily into how well they learn to mask their neurodivergence at such an early age. Emotional dysregulation is sometimes seen as 'normal' in girls because of our sexist stereotypes about girls being hysterical, dramatic or overly emotional. So, you can see that patriarchy is feeding directly into how we deal with neurodivergency.

In the same way that Tema Okun broke down White supremacy culture into a list of characteristics that we explored earlier in the chapter, Professor Walby argues that patriarchy operates through **six unique structures** – which, as you will see, affect how we define what is 'normal' executive functioning, and conversely what we consider to be 'dysfunctional'. Similarly to how we delved into each of the characteristics of White supremacy culture above, I'm going to share four of these structures, explain their meaning in my own words, and explore the ways these have impacted the societal standards, norms and expectations held around executive functioning. (The remaining structures that I won't include are Male Violence and Patriarchal Relations in Sexuality. Both are very real and have very serious implications; however, Male Violence isn't directly linked to our views on 'normal' executive functioning, and we'll touch slightly on Patriarchal Relations in Sexuality later on in **Chapter 3: Inhibition/impulse control, page 133.**)

It's worth pointing out before we begin that these systems don't only marginalize women, but also deeply affect all people who are marginalized for their gender, such as trans women and non-binary folks. However, much more research needs to be done into the impact on these people. On top of this, patriarchy particularly impacts women and people marginalized for their gender who have intersecting identities and are marginalized by multiple systems of oppression, for example, Black women, disabled women and people from poor or working-class backgrounds.

1. Paid work

As I touched on above, women, on average, are still paid considerably less than men for doing the same work. In the UK, 79% of gender pay gap reporting employers stated that median hourly pay in their organization was higher for men than for women. There also continues to be a very prominent **glass**

ceiling – a term, coined by Marilyn Loden in 1978, which refers to the sometimes-invisible barrier to success that many women come up against in their career, meaning that women are less likely to be promoted to senior or managerial roles. Women currently only account for 8.2% of CEO roles in large companies, and it was only in 2023 that the total number of female CEOs of S&P 500 businesses overtook the number of CEOs called John.

How differences in paid work influence how we feel we 'should' behave:

As women and people marginalized for their gender are less likely to hold more senior positions within businesses, this means that they are also less likely to have teams working under them who might support them with tasks that require executive functioning skills like organization, planning, prioritization and flexibility. This means that a woman's difficulties with these tasks might be more obvious, since nobody else is there to fill in the gaps in her skills. For example, if a male CEO struggles with organization, this task might be taken care of by his team or personal assistant, and therefore his struggles wouldn't be as apparent. Whereas if a woman in a more entry-level role has these same organizational difficulties, it is less likely that there would be a support system in place to help her, and therefore these struggles are more likely to be noticeable and have an impact on the work that she is able to complete or the way she is able to 'perform'.

2. Production relations in the household
As of now, in stereotypical, patriarchal, neuronormative relationships, marriages and families,

women are still expected to take on the vast majority of unpaid labour, which Walby describes as being 'under the expectations of her husband'. Research from the Office of National Statistics has shown that on average, men do sixteen hours a week unpaid work, which includes adult care and childcare, laundry and cleaning, compared to twenty-six hours of unpaid work a week done by women.

How production relations in the household influence how we feel we 'should' behave:

Similarly to the workplace example shared above, this same disparity in levels of support can be seen in the home. For example, we might not notice that a man (in a stereotypical, heteronormative relationship) has difficulties with organization, planning and prioritization because these tasks might be taken care of by his wife in her (unpaid) role of 'homemaker'. In addition to this, since women are forced to take on all this additional unpaid labour in the household, they are likely to constantly be spinning a lot more plates, and so it makes sense that some of those plates might fall and crash, and their executive functioning difficulties might be more apparent. Of nine studies that looked specifically at housework as a form of unpaid labour, six reported a relationship between increased housework and poor mental health in women; as our mental health suffers, our ability to 'function normally' is bound to reduce.

We are currently seeing a huge increase in the number of women being diagnosed with ADHD in particular in their thirties, forties, fifties and beyond. We know that a lot of this is down to the fact that the diagnostic criteria for ADHD were not designed to account for the experiences of women, and so they have remained undiagnosed and misdiagnosed for many years, and are also a result of the ways that we are socialized as women to be quiet and polite, and therefore mask many of our ADHD traits. However, could another factor playing into this wave of late diagnoses and realizations be the fact that many of these women, when only having to take care of themselves, had found coping strategies and ways of working around their executive functioning difficulties so that their struggles were not apparent to the people around them, but once they suddenly had a family, husband, children, pets and home to take care of, these coping strategies no longer sufficed and everything came crashing down?

In years gone by, (White) women might not have been expected to work, as they occupied their roles as 'homemakers' and their husbands were the 'sole breadwinners' of the household. However, as feminists have fought for equal rights, and women have (rightly) taken their place in the working world, the expectations held around who is responsible for housework, domestic work, childcare and other care have not kept up with this changing landscape. This means that women have more responsibilities to juggle than ever before, and our executive functioning skills are pushed to their limits. It is, therefore, no wonder that we might be struggling to 'hold things together' in the ways that other undiagnosed neurodivergent people might have done in the past. (It is important to point out that this stereotypical example comes from a place of White privilege, and Black women have historically been enslaved and/or made to work in lower-paid roles while juggling this with their responsibilities as mothers, wives, and/or homemakers.) As **Amy Polly** (she/her), ADHD and mental health speaker and campaigner, explains:

Being diagnosed with ADHD at the age of thirty-seven threw up so many questions. One of the biggest was: **Why now?**

After reflecting on my life and the run-up to my diagnosis, I realized that having my baby was the catalyst for things unravelling. It was at this point in my life that I just had one too many plates to spin, and they all came crashing down.

When I just had myself to look after, it was easy to let the odd plate slip, and dart about between them, and even hide it from the world if one fell. Once I had an extra human to take care of, though, there was just one too many plates to handle.

We have been so conditioned to think that we **must** do it all and do it all well. For those of us who are neurodivergent, there can also be a wave of shame when we feel like we can't. But what I have come to learn, through a process of self-awareness and self-compassion, is that there is, in fact, nothing wrong with me — **but there is, in fact, something wrong with the expectations put upon me.**

It is time to start questioning the plates. It is time to focus on how to spin our own plates. It is time to stop worrying about how others spin their plates. And it's time to start sharing them out.

3. The patriarchal state

The patriarchal state refers to the way that states and countries can be inherently oppressive to women through policies and laws, and that society is fundamentally biased towards men. In Tory Britain, this showed up in austerity measures and budget cuts in social care services, which disproportionately affected women as they often rely more on these services; reductions in funding for healthcare and childcare; policies around parental leave and childcare which often reinforced traditional gender roles; and lack of access to reproductive healthcare, including abortion and contraceptive services, to name but a few.

How the patriarchal state influences how we feel we 'should' behave:

If parental leave policies within businesses and corporations continue to reinforce traditional gender roles, this perpetuates the additional labour assigned to women and people marginalized for their gender, which has the impact discussed above. On top of this, a 2019 study by TODAY found that 52% of women believe that gender discrimination negatively impacts their medical care, and a third of women said they felt a need to 'prove' the legitimacy of their medical concerns and symptoms to their doctors. This means that a woman's or person marginalized for their gender's struggles with executive functioning skills, such as emotional regulation, impulse control and organization, might be seen as 'personal flaws' instead of what they really are – disabling traits.

4. Patriarchal cultural institutions

Many aspects of our culture, such as media, religion and education, produce and perpetuate portrayals of women through a patriarchal viewpoint. For example, there is still a social norm that a man is 'head of the household', or that women are often 'emotional', 'hysterical' or 'irrational'.

How patriarchal cultural institutions influence how we feel we 'should' behave:

As Gina Martin shared above, 'Emotional dysregulation is sometimes seen as "normal" in girls because of our sexist stereotypes about girls being hysterical, dramatic or overly emotional.' Before I was diagnosed as autistic and ADHD, I personally had my emotional regulation difficulties put down to 'hormones', and my social difficulties at school put down to the fact that 'girls could just be bitches sometimes', instead of them being taken seriously as traits of my (undiagnosed) disabilities. In a patriarchal culture, men are socialized to 'man up' and hide their emotions or any display of vulnerability, and women and people marginalized for their gender, while socialized to show their emotions more, are told that, in order to be taken seriously, they must learn to do the same. This leads us to label any display of emotions as 'dysregulated' or 'dysfunctional' when, in reality, those emotions are a perfectly normal, valid and human response to specific circumstances or situations.

Capitalism

Capitalism is defined as an economic and political system in which property, business and industry are controlled by private owners rather than by the state, with the purpose of making a profit. It's the system that defines us by our ability to work, achieve things and, essentially, make money. It puts profit ahead of people; ahead of our happiness, health, comfort and fulfilment. This affects our relationship with executive functioning in a number of different ways:

- **Over-valuing productivity**
  In a capitalist system, efficiency and productivity are considered to be two of the most important things, since these are the means to achieving the material wealth that is prioritized under capitalism. This means that we're encouraged to strive for more, bigger, and better, and told that our ability to achieve things in a workplace environment will help us get there. If we didn't place so much importance on productivity and success, we wouldn't need to plan, prioritize, hold and manipulate information, or initiate tasks immediately in the ways we are currently expected to.

- **Over-valuing independence**
  Under capitalism, each person is seen as an individual working part, rather than cogs working together as part of a bigger machine. We're expected to be completely independent, and so any interdependence or reliance on community or support is considered

as 'weak', or something to be ashamed of. Executive functioning differences such as challenges with planning, impulsivity or disorganization are seen as personal shortcomings, rather than considering that we might just need support or input from the people around us. Humans have always relied on their 'tribe', but capitalism rejects this notion and reinforces the expectation that we should be 100% self-fulfilling and self-sufficient.

- **Access to support**
  In the UK we have seen the Tory Government repeatedly cut funding to education, healthcare, and social care and services, which has made it increasingly difficult for people to access the support, resources and accommodations that they need to be able to 'function' in the ways that society deems normal. With the proper support and resources, many of the things that we consider to be 'dysfunctional' would not cause half as much suffering. For example, does this person have 'emotional dysregulation', or can they just not access therapy to process and work through a difficult experience? Does this person struggle with 'working memory', or, if they had access to support tools like a dictaphone in the workplace, would this struggle go away? Does this person struggle with planning and prioritization, or are they just having to spin an impossible amount of plates while they work three jobs in order to support themself and their family?

- **Marketing and consumerism**

  Just like the way that the beauty industry was designed
  to make us feel we need to buy certain products to
  be desirable, capitalism creates 'problems' in order
  to be able to provide (and market) 'solutions' to those
  problems, which drive the economy. It reframes natural
  differences in ways of being as problems that 'need
  fixing', because if we believe that we need to be fixed,
  we are more likely to be swayed to buy whatever is
  promising to 'fix' us. As much as some apps, products
  and services will genuinely help us work with our brains
  rather than against them, some might capitalize on our
  feelings of being 'wrong', 'bad' or 'inadequate'.

Colonialism

Colonialism is defined as 'control by one power over a dependent area or people'. As *National Geographic* explains, 'colonialism occurs when one nation subjugates another, conquering its population and exploiting it, often while forcing its own language and cultural values upon its people'.

Historically, the British Empire, along with other predominantly White European nations, colonized countries and communities across the globe, with many nations still under the rule of colonialism, and an even greater number still feeling the implications. When these predominantly White colonizers imposed their control over different nations, they forced their own ways of being, thinking, behaving and working on the native people, and tried to extract as much profit and labour from these colonized lands and people as possible, instead of respecting their heritage and traditional cultures. The effects of this rule still live on in our framing of executive functioning to this day. I spoke to my wonderful friend **Kelechi Okafor** (she/her), Black-British actress, director, author and public speaker, about this, and she explained:

> There is a place in Lagos called 'Surulere'. I've always found this name interesting because loosely translated to English, it means '**patience has worth**'. To me, it speaks of a time before rampant British colonialism, which brought Nigeria as we know it into being.
>
> Colonialism deftly reflects how society treats atypical thinkers and doers.
>
> Firstly, what is known as Nigeria today is a forced amalgamation of various ethnic groups. The ways these groups lived were unique and special. Through the depraved colonial lens, lines were drawn through lands and people forced together, languages disregarded, with English inflicted as the main source of communication. **Of course it would cause dysregulation.**
>
> Sound familiar? When society ignores our individual way of processing the world and forces all of us under one mode of thinking/doing as a means of

aiming to extract the most amount of labour from us, **we are bound to feel untethered.**

Why did I mention Surulere? Because as an area named by the Yoruba ethnic group of Nigeria, it clearly identifies a time when patience was seen as worthy and time wasn't wound around our throats as a threat.

Colonialism is integral to modern-day working practices because to dominate a country, one must first flatten all that makes that country unique; thus, all the resources can be extracted from that country while the country has been made to believe such debilitating extraction is for its own good. That's how the working environment and various professional industries function: asking that neurodivergence be left aside and our experiences flattened to the point that our aim is to keep up with a society that only intends to leave us behind.

Society demands endless labour through a very specific framework, which disallows individual modes of working because various individuals can't be controlled, but a homogenous group can. Thus to make our uniqueness appear unprofessional would mean that peer pressure forces us into confinement and away from our creativity and self-worth.

Ableism

Ableism is a form of discrimination or prejudice against disabled people based on the incorrect and harmful belief that disabled people are 'inferior' or 'less capable' than non-disabled people. It involves the marginalization, stigmatization and exclusion of disabled people in many aspects of life, including education, employment, social interactions and access to support. Ableism can show up through stereotypes (such as that disabled people are 'lazy'), misconceptions (such as feeling sympathy towards disabled people), or the denial of rights and opportunities (such as unemployment). All these things ultimately hinder disabled people from being able to fully participate and be included in society.

These ableist ideas have a huge impact on what we consider to be 'normal' executive functioning vs 'executive dysfunction' because, instead of seeing differences in the ways that disabled people might need (or choose) to do things as a neutral part of human variation, we see them as 'wrong' or 'lesser'. I asked **Rachel Charlton-Dailey** (she/they), disabled editor, journalist and activist, how this had affected her, and she explained:

> Ableism subconsciously underpins so much of what we think of as 'normal' in society – and especially work. This can be from working in-person being seen as the 'only right way' to work when many need to work from home, to people being criticized for 'fidgeting' when

they're actually stimming (repeated movements, actions or sounds done by a neurodivergent person to self-stimulate or self-regulate) . When the world has been built by mostly non-disabled and neurotypical people, anything they don't experience is seen as being 'weird' or, worse, invalid.

The way the media has portrayed disabled (and especially neurodivergent) people as either human computers or ditzy, flaky job-jumpers means that we see executive functions as problems instead of things that can be worked around and incorporated. We see emotional dysregulation as 'hysterical women' or, more recently, 'snowflakes'; lack of organization or planning is seen as being bad at your job; and lateness or memory issues are seen as not caring. Ableism and ableist views keep so many neurodivergent people from living up to their full potential because they're written off for things they can't change. In reality, it's not the neurodivergent person that is the problem; society's problem in supporting them is.

Cathy Reay (she/her), disabled journalist and author, shares a great example of this:

Here's something I haven't admitted publicly before: I mostly work from my bed. I send emails in bed, and I take calls from my bed, throwing up an underwater background to hide my pillows in Teams meetings so people won't know.

I'm living the dream, right?

But then, why don't I tell people?

Because even I still wrestle with my inner ableist voice telling me I've failed because I haven't managed to power walk around an office building and sit in an unbearably uncomfortable chair. And if I think I have no excuse for working from my bed, what are non-disabled people going to think?!

Ableism is entrenched so deeply into the fabric of our society that we all – even disabled people ourselves – struggle with identifying disability as a legitimate reason for working or doing things differently. We attribute value and importance to people based on how busy they are (or are perceived to be) and on how much they get done. Kim Kardashian's famous line 'Get your fucking ass up and work. It seems like nobody wants to work these days' caused uproar when she said it, but she was only voicing the ideas our society promotes – a hustle-and-grind culture that fails so many of us in disabled, neurodivergent and sick communities.

Truth is, whether I work from bed or not is irrelevant to my worth, both as an employee and as a human being. If we need to do things differently, need support, or take longer to complete tasks, that doesn't mean we're unqualified or somehow not as good as others. It means we're doing our best, and that's all we can do.

Charli Clement (they/she) expands on this same point in their book *All Tangled Up in Autism and Chronic Illness*, where they explain, 'For those of us struggling with chronic fatigue and pain when at an uncomfortable desk, the option of working in bed means that we can at least do *some* work, where not doing so might mean we cannot do anything.'

—

Recap

Overall, we can see that these biases and systems of oppression (including but not limited to White supremacy, capitalism, patriarchy, colonialism and ableism) inform our culture and, obviously, therefore have an impact on how we perceive executive functioning, and therefore how we 'should' behave. We think that not being able to initiate a task immediately is 'bad' because it is deemed important under capitalist systems where productivity is a priority, and we think that outward displays of emotion are 'wrong' because patriarchy tells us that they are weak. What is considered to be 'dysfunctional' is not objective, there is no definitive 'right' or 'wrong' when it comes to human behaviour and thinking styles; what is 'normal' or 'dysfunctional' is subjective – and ill-informed by harmful biases. Although we cannot individually dismantle these systems of oppression (and the responsibility absolutely shouldn't rely on marginalized people to do so), we can begin to find ways of working, functioning, behaving, living and being that better suit **ALL** of us. By questioning what has always been considered the 'right' way of doing things, or the way we 'should' do things, we can start to make more space for people beyond the privileged few who have traditionally held the power.

In this chapter, we have explored:

- Which **systems of oppression** have impacted the way we think about executive functioning.

- How these systems define what is considered 'normal' vs 'disordered'.

- What we can do to begin to resist these systems of oppression.

Your takeaway box

- All of us, however marginalized or privileged, have grown up and been socialized in a society which holds many harmful biases. It is not our fault that we have been conditioned to hold certain incorrect beliefs about how we should behave, live and exist, which directly affect the way we perceive neurodivergent people. However, it is our responsibility to do the work to begin to change those beliefs. The best starting point is to listen to those with lived experience of these biases, especially those whose intersecting identities mean that they are marginalized by multiple systems of oppression.

- We don't need to be experts in each and every system of oppression, but once we start to understand the fact that these systems exist and impact our society's norms and expectations, we can start to question whether those norms and expectations actually matter at all and let go of any shame we might have felt for not being able to meet them. It's only when we let go of how we *should* be that we can truly be ourselves.

- Once we are able to shift some of the emphasis that we've put on 'the way that things have always been done' being the only and correct way of doing things, we can start to look for different and better ways to function in our day-to-day lives, which are more suited to each of us.

1

Working memory

As an undiagnosed teenager, my **all-time** favourite quote was a line from Augustus Waters's final letter in **The Fault in Our Stars** by John Green. Augustus wants to write something special for his friend Hazel Grace but is struggling to get his words to work in the way that he wants them to (something I'm sure many of us here can relate to!), so he attempts to enlist the help of her favourite author. In his letter to the author explaining his situation and asking for help, Augustus writes: '**My thoughts are stars I can't fathom into constellations.**' To undiagnosed, chaotic, all-over-the-place Ellie, this idea rang truer than almost anything I'd ever heard. It's a metaphor I still love to use to this day.

However, in addition to being stars I can't fathom into constellations, my thoughts appear to be something else, too: **balloons I can't seem to hold down.** This second metaphor is one I've adopted since getting my ADHD diagnosis to explain just how difficult it can be to keep hold of all the many ideas floating around my brain. I feel as though each thought, idea, important piece of information, date, appointment, meeting and task in my brain is a helium balloon. It is desperate to float away into the sky unless I am consciously making the effort to hold it down – and I am aware that if I **do** ever lose my grip, it will fly away, never to be seen again. However, holding all these balloons in my hands all the time can be tricky; it takes up a lot of energy and takes away from my capacity to do the other things that I need to do.

In this chapter, we will explore:

- What is working memory?
- Which systems have affected the way we think about working memory?
- How can we support ourselves with working memory?
- 5 things to consider putting in place for your working memory.

Learning to work with our brains rather than against them is all about finding the balance between letting go of the neuronormative 'shoulds' that don't serve us, and finding ways to support ourselves in doing the things that do.

If we can reduce the pressure we are under by trying to find environments in which we can safely unmask, and generally get a wider range of our needs met, we can free up some capacity and have a little bit more room to breathe.

What is working memory?

Our first executive functioning skill, **working memory**, is explained as the ability to **hold and manipulate information for short-term use**. This includes tasks such as remembering a phone number, asking for directions and recalling them for the duration of our journey, and learning the name of someone new and being able to remember it throughout the conversation. Unlike long-term memories that are retained even when we're not thinking of them, working memory is more like a mental notepad (or person holding balloons!) that keeps hold of all the information we currently need.

There are different estimates about the 'normal' capacity of someone's working memory. In a 1956 paper famously describing 'the magical number seven plus or minus two', Miller demonstrated that 'one can repeat back a list of no more than about seven randomly ordered, meaningful items or chunks (which could be letters, digits, or words)'. Other research has suggested that young adults can recall only three or four longer verbal chunks, such as idioms or short sentences.

Everyone can struggle with working memory sometimes; I'm sure every single person in the world has come back from the supermarket and realized that they've forgotten something important, walked into a room and forgotten what they came in for, forgotten the name of a friend-of-a-friend, or lost track of what they were trying to say mid-way through a sentence. However, for ADHDers, autistic people, and other neurodivergent people whose executive functioning skills work slightly differently, these occurrences are much more frequent. I often refer to my brain (another metaphor, I think this might be a theme throughout the book!) as being like a sieve – because the information seems to come into my mind and then pour straight through.

In a 2020 study into working memory and short-term memory deficits in ADHD (we're not huge fans of the word 'deficits' around here, but that's the name of the paper!), Kofler et al. found that 'ADHD status was associated with very large magnitude impairments in central executive working memory . . . and these deficits covaried with ADHD inattentive and hyperactive/impulsive symptom severity based on both parent and teacher report.' I'm not a fan of the way this is worded, as I prefer to refer to my experiences as 'differences' or 'traits' rather than symptoms, and 'severity' isn't always the best way of measuring somebody's experience because it doesn't account for what's going on internally or the level of masking that's occurring. That being said, I find Kofler's discovery that **no matter how much somebody's traits of hyperactivity or inattention present outwardly, it is likely that they will have a marked difference in their working memory** incredibly interesting to consider.

One explanation for this is that ADHDers (or people who are otherwise neurodivergent) are already using more of their working memory at any given time just to be able to work, live, socialize and communicate in a world that was not built with our needs in mind. For example, as we can struggle with auditory processing, we are constantly having to work harder to listen to and process any information that is presented to us verbally, which takes away from our total working memory capacity. If we think of the earlier example of being able to juggle seven things (or balls) at any one time, one of these balls is already being taken up by auditory processing, and others might also be used for things like masking, forcing eye contact, suppressing stims and staying focused. This means that we have fewer 'available balls' to *actually* hold and manipulate the information that we need to. Neurodivergent people constantly have to **actively** work to process information, mask, stay focused and be organized – things that tend to be 'simple' for others, or to be considered 'a given' – and so, naturally, that takes away from our capacity to be spinning multiple plates all at the same time.

Which systems have affected the way we think about working memory?

As with all the executive functions we will explore throughout the book, although the ability to hold and manipulate information is necessary to a *certain extent*, the ways in which we currently consider 'deficits' in working memory are a social construct defined by neuronormative standards. As Spaeth and Pearson explained in their research on neurodiversity and student well-being, 'being able to hold a more limited amount of information in working memory is not disabling if one has access to tools like a Dictaphone'.

Who said that we need to be able to remember seven things at any given time to be a functioning member of society?

Who said that we had to be able to manipulate any and all information on the spot and couldn't write it down or take a bit of time to process it?

Who said that we needed to be able to interpret verbal instructions and couldn't request information in a written or visual format?

Many of the ways that we are disabled by our differences in working memory are, in reality, just down to the way that our neuronormative, capitalist society has functioned up until this point. In the simplest terms, it's more efficient (and therefore makes businesses more money) if we can juggle multiple bits of information at any one time . . . but, aside from that, it doesn't *actually* have any sort of moral or definitive superiority. Capitalism has hugely contributed to shaping the way that working memory is perceived and valued because it emphasizes its importance for productivity, adaptability and competitive success in a constantly changing economic landscape. However, if we didn't define people's worth based on their ability to be productive, it wouldn't matter so much if they couldn't multitask or switch between tasks easily; they could, instead, just focus on one thing (that brought them enjoyment and fulfilment, or that they felt warranted their attention at that moment, rather than what made the most profit) at a time.

Another of the ways that society defines what we 'should' be able to manage with our working memory is **individualism**, outlined as one of Tema Okun's characteristics of **White supremacy culture** (see **What defines our view of executive functioning?, page 19**).

Individualism shows up in the belief that each person demands to be seen (or is told that they must be seen) as a **completely independent individual**, without acknowledging the ways that they interact with the society and community around them. On the one hand, individualism explains the way that many people struggle to work as a team and want individual credit and recognition for their personal achievements rather than being happy to play a part in the bigger picture. The other side of this means that individualism also reinforces the idea that we all must be able to exist completely independently, without support from the people around us. It values **independence over interdependence** and **self-sufficiency over community and collaboration**. This is particularly unhelpful for those who have differences in their executive functioning skills, such as neurodivergent and disabled people, as it makes us feel inadequate for being reliant on care or support from our families, friends, partners or the system, instead of realizing that human beings **need** connection. Ever since our cave-person days, we have always relied on a tribe of people around us – and that should not change now.

Some examples of the ways individualism affects the way we see working memory and executive functioning:

- Each person is expected to be able to 'function' and manage every single thing they encounter in life completely independently, which means that anybody who has any support needs is deemed to be 'disordered'.

- We are seen as incompetent if we need to rely on support in remembering everything all at once or juggling multiple tasks or projects – whether this is from the people around us or by using tools like digital reminders or writing things down. In reality, there is no real problem with relying on these things.

- We are expected to be able to remember every step
  of a task without assistance, which puts a much
  greater strain on our working memory, and complete
  projects and tasks independently, which also puts a
  much greater strain on planning, prioritization and task
  initiation (other executive functions that we'll come to
  in later chapters).

Also, closely linked with individualism, and typical of neuronorma-tive society, is another characteristic of White supremacy culture: **I'm the Only One**. This describes the belief many people hold that, if they want something done 'right', they have to be the ones to do it themselves. Despite knowing that I am disabled, I am defin-itely guilty of holding this belief; I can really struggle to let things out of my control, and feel as though I've got to do everything myself, instead of realizing that there are hundreds and thousands of people out there who are just as capable as I am and finding ways of delegating to someone else! This belief might cause all of us to feel that we need to micro-manage, struggle with delegation and idolize 'leaders' or 'public figures'. Instead, we need to recognize that there is no moral value in taking everything on yourself and that no one is superior for doing so.

How I'm the Only One affects the way we see working memory and executive functioning:

- Since we struggle to delegate, we end up with an
  enormous amount of work to complete independently.
  If this work was distributed between several people, it

wouldn't matter if one person struggled with planning, for example, as somebody else would be able to fill in the gaps in this area.

- This idea of feeling like we are the 'Only One' might translate to thinking we are the only person experiencing things the way we do, or struggling the way we are, which means we might not understand that the people around us also face similar struggles.

- Individuals may believe that their challenges are unique and that no one else will understand them or be able to support them. This means that they are less likely to seek support from the people around them.

It's important to remember all of this as we explore the following tips and strategies for supporting our working memory, as the **last** thing that we want to be doing is putting unnecessary pressure on ourselves to remember **every single detail all of the time**. These tips are designed to help you to do and remember the things that you **need** to, but it's equally important that we work out which things we **actually** need to do or remember. Learning to work with our brains rather than against them is all about finding the balance between letting go of the neuronormative 'shoulds' that don't serve us and finding ways to support ourselves in doing the things that do.

How can we support ourselves with working memory?

When considering the things that we can do to support ourselves with these working memory struggles (or differences), it is helpful to consider all the extra things that we are constantly juggling, like masking and auditory processing, that we touched on earlier in the chapter. If we can reduce the pressure we are under by trying to find environments in which we can safely unmask, access information in written rather than verbal formats, and generally get a wider range of our needs met, we can free up some of this capacity for our working memory to have a little bit more room to breathe. For example, in the context of a workplace setting, if employees are constantly using up brain space and energy by monitoring and adapting the ways that they work and behave to conform to a culture that doesn't suit them, this takes away from the brain space and energy that they have available to actually get the job done.

Further to this, not only are we using up our capacity on things like auditory processing and masking, but because of these things, we might also be using up even more of our capacity on something else – anxiety. In the words of **Professor John Amaechi OBE** (he/him), *New York Times* bestselling author of *The Promises of Giants*, 'We each have a finite amount of energy to spend each day. Holding onto feelings of anxiety – when we feel we have to hide our true selves – uses up some of that limited energy. When we feel real inclusion, our anxiety levels reduce again, and if that energy is not being used on anxiety, it can be dedicated to progress.' When we are supported and accommodated by the people around us, or when we learn to better accommodate ourselves, we can take away some of that anxiety, freeing up some more of our working memory capacity.

If we also think back to the 'helium balloon' metaphor that I like to use for the things in our brain which constantly feel as though they're going to fly away, we can use this idea to help us consider some of the things that we can do to help with our working memory. If someone was struggling to hold on to so many balloons all at once, we have a couple of options that might help. First, we could tie some of those balloons to a stand (make a note of them somewhere or have some way of keeping them in place in our minds). Equally, we could pass the balloon to somebody else to hold on to for a while (by delegating certain tasks or reminders either to the people around us or to technology like our phones and laptops).

Before we get into the meatier strategies, tips and tricks, I want to quickly set the scene by reminding you of a list of things that are **absolutely fine** (and might help with your working memory). So many of the things that would take **so much** weight off our shoulders are teeny, tiny adjustments that we are well within our rights to do or ask for – we've just been conditioned, because of those pesky societal norms, to think that we shouldn't. However, as you know, the aim is to **let go** of those shoulds, so you can find ways that you **CAN**.

A list of things that are <u>absolutely fine</u>:

- Asking for instructions, deadlines and tasks to be confirmed in a written rather than verbal format.

- Asking for an email with a summary of notes and actions to be sent to follow up a call or meeting.

- Asking for a verbal debriefing or list of instructions after a call or meeting.

- Asking for all communication to be streamlined to one medium or format, e.g. one singular email chain, so you can go back and check details.

- Using a dictaphone, notepad, or the notes app on your phone to keep track of information as and when you receive it rather than trying to juggle it all mentally.

- Relying on alarms or notifications to remind you of important tasks like when to take your medication, appointments or meetings.

- Telling your friends, family and colleagues to 'feel free to nudge me if I haven't done this/followed up about this/got back to you' within a certain amount of time.

- Ordering your supermarket shopping online rather than having to remember everything while you're in-store.

- Repeating instructions back to somebody to make sure that you've processed or remembered them correctly.

- Jotting down notes or underlining or highlighting text while reading.

- Talking out loud about something that you're reading to process it verbally and cement it in your mind.

- Relying on multiple senses to process information, e.g. following captions while you listen to a TV show, or listening to an audiobook while also reading it on the page.

Fun fact: One thing that society has tweaked to suit our working memory (in some parts of the world) is the way that we write or recite long strings of numbers, like phone numbers or national insurance/social security numbers. In the US, they use hyphens to separate the phone numbers into smaller groups, and in the UK we usually use the framework of (this is a tricky one to explain in black and white, so bear with me!):

07123 *breath* 456 *breath* 789

This is because it's easier to remember a few small groups of numbers (a group of 5, a group of 3, and a group of 3) than it is to remember one long string of numbers. Pretty cool, huh? This could also help to explain why it can be so difficult for us to compute when somebody reads our number back to us using a different structure or framework; we don't store the phone number in our brain as one whole 'thing'; we store it as three disconnected groups of numbers.

Tip 1:
Mastering your to-do

A big part of learning to work *with* your working memory, rather than against it, is finding ways to transfer some of the busyness and spinning plates out of your brain and on to or into some sort of tangible storage solution. Think of the idea of tying some of those helium balloons on to a balloon stand rather than trying to hold on to them all at once! This not only makes sure that important pieces of information are stored somewhere (and are therefore at less risk of floating away or being forgotten about), but also helps to relieve some of the overwhelm of having hundreds of thoughts, ideas, and things to remember constantly buzzing around in your brain. I've often seen ADHDers refer to having 'bees in their brain' (which I can definitely relate to!), and if we use that metaphor, we're removing some of the swarm from the hive and separating them into different compartments where they all have a bit more space to relax.

The most traditional way that people tend to go about this is by using a to-do list, and, in this (rare!) case, I surprisingly agree with the 'norm' – I just think it needs a little bit of tweaking to better suit the way that our brains tend to *actually* work.

The traditional to-do list has a few main faults that I'd like to address:

- First, it doesn't help with prioritization (we'll touch on this more in **Chapter 6: Planning and prioritization,**

page 236). It is just one long list of tasks that, although helping to get all the different tasks out of our brains, can still feel pretty overwhelming.

- Linked to this, it's often not very visually appealing. A long list of words, maybe with a tick box if you're lucky, and that's about all. There is very little colour, organization, or visual structure involved.

- We've also got really good (thanks to, you guessed it, those pesky societal expectations) at tying a lot of **shame** to our to-do lists. We'll pile every single thing we think we 'should' do on there, which ends up being a monumental list of things that would be physically impossible to get through, and then feel like we've 'failed' if we haven't managed to tick everything off at the end of the day. This might lead to us actually *avoiding* writing things down because we don't want to be confronted with all that stuff we're 'supposed' to try (and most likely fail) to get through.

- If you struggle with object impermanence or object constancy, like many ADHDers, in particular, do (only remembering something exists when it is directly in front of you, and forgetting its existence completely when it's out of sight, out of mind – which we'll touch on more later in this chapter), it's likely you'll write things on a list somewhere, put that list down, and then forget that the list itself actually exists. Helpful!

- Finally, especially if you're an ADHDer like me, it can be tricky to keep track of every to-do all in one place. You might have Post-it notes, a desk planner, a list in your phone notes app, a shopping list on the fridge, an online list like Notion or Monday, an app like Tiimo, and a couple of different notebooks all on the go, all at once. (This feels a lot like the popular Spiderman meme that you might have seen online, where all the different identical Spidermen are pointing at each other . . . Except it's just me and my silly little brain, being confronted with the fact that I *still* often actually have all these lists in progress at once, and then wonder why I struggle with feeling overwhelmed. Oops.)

Essentially, like with all the tips I'll share throughout the book, it's about finding what works for **you**, but there are a few different things I'd like to share with you to consider when **mastering your to-do**:

1. One framework I particularly like, and that I've been workshopping recently, is splitting your to-do list into the following sections:

    – **Must do:** Things that **need** (like, *actually* need) to get done.

    – **Could do:** Things that it would be **good** if you got done, but the world won't end if you don't.

    – **To dump or delegate:** Things that either need doing but don't need to be done by you specifically and therefore can be **passed to someone else**, or things that can be **crossed off** the list completely.

– **To do later:** Those balloons that you need to tie down somewhere to be dealt with or remembered for later but that don't need to be thought about today.

I find the '**To do later**' section particularly helpful because it allows me to take all those different bits and bobs I'm clinging on to and put them down somewhere, but without overwhelming myself by having them all added on to the end of my working to-do list, which makes it seem like they're all things currently on my plate at this very moment. You can try this framework using the template on the following page, and we've also created a notepad that uses this design that you can find at **weareunmasked.com**.

2. Another framework that **Grace Beverley** (she/her), founder of TALA, Shreddy & The Productivity Method, shares in her book ***Working Hard, Hardly Working*** and uses in her Productivity Planners separates things out in a slightly different way. She suggests using:

– **Quick ticks:** Things that can be done in under 5 minutes.

– **Tasks:** Things that will take between 5 and 30 minutes.

– **Projects:** Things that will take over 30 minutes.

This perhaps helps more with **prioritization and planning**, which we'll explore more in **Chapter 6 (page 236)**, but is still a nifty way of getting all of that busyness out of your brain and on to paper.

3. Something that is very important for those of us who struggle with object impermanence, or 'out of sight, out of mind', is having our to-do list in a very obvious and easily locatable place. Two options I like for this are using a notepad over a desk planner (as you can carry it around in your bag and therefore have it with you at all times) or, if you prefer using an app or digital to-do list rather than paper, using Widgets on your smartphone. These Widgets pin your to-do list to your home screen so that every time you pick up and unlock your phone (which, let's face it, for most of us with busy brains is *many, many* times a day), the list will be right there staring back at you. As well as keeping your to-do list front of mind, these methods also make sure that your lists are easy to access, meaning that all of those balloons are tied somewhere safe – but equally somewhere that you can access them whenever you need to.

<u>Must do</u>	**<u>Could do</u>**
–	–
–	–
–	–
–	–
–	–
–	–
<u>To dump or delegate</u>	**<u>To do later</u>**
–	–
–	–
–	–
–	–
–	–
–	–

Tip 2:
Share to cement

Research shows that one of the best ways to cement something that you've learned in your brain is to teach that information to somebody else.

In two experiments, two groups of participants were asked to study some material. The first group was told that they would then teach that material to another student before being tested, and the second group were told that they would only be tested.

The result? The group of students who were told that they would need to teach the information to somebody else had **better free recall** of the material and also **correctly answered more questions** about the material. According to the researchers, 'When teachers prepare to teach, they tend to seek out key points and organize information into a coherent structure. Our results suggest that students also turn to these types of effective learning strategies when they expect to teach.'

Similarly, in a recent experiment, people were taught about the Doppler effect (the phenomenon that causes the siren on a police car to be high-pitched as it approaches you and lower-pitched as it passes you). At the end of the study, the participants all had to deliver a lesson on the material – but half of them were allowed to use notes, and half of them had to deliver the lesson without notes. A week later, they all came back and had to take a surprise test on the information that they had learned. The study found that the people who had taught the lesson **without notes** did better than those who were allowed to use notes to support them. Having to explain what they had learned in their own words meant that the information better stuck in their brain.

As **Adam Grant** (he/him), organizational psychologist and bestselling author, explains in an article for the *New York Times*: 'The best way to learn something truly is to teach it – not just because **explaining** it helps you **understand** it, but also because **retrieving** it helps you **remember** it.'

So, what does that mean for those of us who struggle with working memory? Well, we can find different ways of teaching (or sharing) information with somebody else in order to make it stick in our brains.

What structures could I put in place to help Share to Cement?

Here are some ideas to get you started:

- I could find a study partner to meet up with and share what I've been working on or learning.

- I could share my to-do list with an accountability partner every morning to help cement it in my brain (this added accountability has the double effect of making you more likely to get the things you've shared done, too, since you want to uphold a 'good' impression to this person!).

- I could tell my partner or housemates what
  I've done or learned throughout the day
  over dinner to help cement those things in
  my mind.

- _____
  _____
  _____

- _____
  _____
  _____

- _____
  _____
  _____

- _____
  _____
  _____

Tip 3:
Showroom chic

As we touched on in **Tip 1: Mastering your to-do**, ADHDers, especially, can be prone to experiencing a serious case of 'out of sight, out of mind'. This is because we experience differences in object permanence, also referred to as object constancy.

Object permanence means having the understanding that items and people still exist even when you can't see or hear them. This concept was coined by child psychologist Jean Piaget and is an important milestone in a baby's brain development. As I explained in *unmasked*:

> If you're playing peek-a-boo with a one-year-old,
> they are endlessly entertained because, to them,
> when you're hidden behind something, you cease
> to exist. Then – peek-a-boo! – you spontaneously
> reappear. How exciting! But if you were playing
> that same game with a four-year-old, it doesn't
> have the same appeal; because their object
> permanence has developed, they know that you're
> just hiding and that, even when they can't see you,
> you still exist.

In a similar phenomenon, ADHDers can struggle with **object constancy**, meaning that if something isn't in our immediate view, we forget that it exists. For me, this often looks like putting something in a 'safe place', forgetting that it exists for a while, forgetting where that safe place is once I need the thing, and then getting *very* agitated when I can't find it. My mum often makes the observation that I look like a cartoon character ripping everything out of a suitcase and launching it behind them when I am looking for something!

Being 'tidy' (read: keeping things hidden away in cupboards) just doesn't work for the way that our brains work. We need to rip up the idea that for your house to be 'presentable', everything needs to be stored out of sight (leaving no visible evidence that somebody *actually* lives in the space) and replace it with a system that better reminds our brains of the things we **need**, the things we want to **get done**, and the things we **have**. One way to do this is to start treating your home like a personal showroom — less minimalism, more **showroom chic**!

To work around my struggles with object constancy, I now keep the things I need in obvious places:

- My keys live on a hook right next to the front door rather than in a drawer.

- Any ongoing paperwork or post lives in a tray on top of the fridge so that each time I go to the fridge, I'm reminded that it needs to be dealt with.

- My gym and work bags live on hooks in the corridor, rather than me having to remember to pack them and pick them up every time I leave the house.

- My daily medication is kept on the kitchen counter to prompt me to take it when I'm making my breakfast.

Keeping things on show helps to regularly prompt your brain of their existence and importance, rather than constantly using up energy when thinking, 'I must remember to take my medication in the morning,' or, 'I must remember to pick up my gym bag when I leave for work.' Bonus points for having it visible **and** in a convenient place for the task it ties to, like my example of keeping my ADHD meds next to the toaster so I remember to have them with breakfast! You can use the template below to brainstorm some of the things you could put on show to make life a little easier for yourself.

Important thing	Where I could put it on show

Tip 4:
Master directory

In **Tip 3: Showroom chic**, we thought about how we could keep some of the things we need to remember on show in our homes to give our brains a little nudge that they exist, or need dealing with, or need picking up before we leave the house. However, for some important things, this doesn't work as easily.

As an example, how many times have we all laid awake at night wondering, 'Where the heck is my passport?' or, 'When did I last see my birth certificate?' If you're anything like me, then the answer is probably: **many**. However, in these cases, leaving things on display isn't the best solution to the problem; we can hardly keep our most important and confidential documents pinned up along our walls! (Or maybe we could, who am I to start imposing new shouldn'ts and couldn'ts!)

For smaller, more important things like these, I like to use the idea of a **master directory**. This could be a spreadsheet saved on your computer, a note saved on your phone, or a list kept in a notepad (stored somewhere you won't forget!) that records the whereabouts of each of those important things. This might look like:

Important thing	Where it's stored
Passport	In the top drawer of my bedside table
Birth certificate	In the blue folder on the shelf in the spare room
Spare car key	In the pink box in the cutlery drawer

As much as we might like to *think* that we don't need this list, and that this time we ***absolutely definitely positively*** will remember exactly where we've put the thing, the reality is that having a written log of these lists is going to be a much better solution for keeping track than relying on our busy brains. It also frees up some brain space (remember the 'seven things' concept from the start of the chapter) so that the energy that was previously being used in remembering where each of the important things was being kept can be freed up and used for something more useful.

The more specific you can be with your answers, the better – and the fewer different places you have to store important bits and bobs, the easier it will be to keep track of! You can fill out your own list on the template below (you can either copy this out into your diary or notebook, or remember to keep this book somewhere you'll be able to find it later!).

Important thing	Where it's stored

Tip 5:
Prep your launch pad

One of the ways that my working memory catches me out the most is the fact that I will pretty much **always** forget something that I need when leaving the house, whether it's my purse, my notepad, my camera, my gym bag, my deodorant, a parcel I needed to drop off at the Post Office, or (most frequently, as my brother Lewis will know and often likes to remind me) my phone charger. If we think back to the idea that people can remember seven different things at once, then it's no wonder remembering each of these things every time we leave the house doesn't go particularly well, especially for those of us who have differences in our working memory capabilities, like autistic people or ADHDers.

One way to work around this is to set yourself up with a **launch pad**: instead of having to remember each individual item every time you leave the house, you have one bag that is **always** packed with everything you need.

If you were on TikTok in the summer of 2023, you might have seen the hype about the Uniqlo cross-body bag – a small but deceivingly spacious handbag that people were amazed at (and loved to show off) just how much they could fit inside. Having a bag like this, with all your must-haves safely stored inside, that's ready to pick up and sling over your shoulder every time you head out – whether that's to work, to meet friends, on a night out, or to the gym – takes the pressure off your working memory to keep track of everything you need. Having extras of these things (e.g. a phone charger that always stays in your bag, rather than having one phone charger that you have to remember to unplug and take with you every morning) means that it's one less thing to worry about. You might want to include:

- A phone charger

- A fidget or stim toy

- Your purse

- Mini toiletries like deodorant or lip balm

- Some earplugs or headphones

By doing this, you can ensure that no matter where you're heading and no matter how late you might be running, you just have to pick up the launch pad and go — and you don't have to worry about any of these important things being left behind. No more rummaging through drawers when you should have left the house ten minutes ago, and no more getting to your destination and face-palming as you realize you've left something you *really need* at home. You can just check in at the launch pad and get ready for take-off!

Things that could live in my launch pad:

- _____

- _____

- _____

- _____

- _____

Bonus tip: If you're a frequent traveller (whether that's with holidays or overnight trips with work), you can apply the same principle for your overnight bag – having a spare toothbrush, razor, pack of make-up wipes and phone charger that always live in your travel bag so that you don't have to remember to pop them in every single time.

Working memory recap

Our first executive function, **working memory**, is defined as the ability to hold and manipulate information for short-term use. It's a necessary tool to be able to keep track of different bits of information and remember all the things we need to; however, as we've explored, there are definitely ways we can reframe what we 'should' be able to manage on our own and put things in place to make things that little bit easier for our brains to keep on top of.

In this chapter, we have explored:

- What working memory is.

- The systems which have affected the way we think about working memory.

- Some ways we can support ourselves with working memory.

- 5 things to consider putting in place for your working memory.

Your takeaway box

- The idea that you need to be able to remember every single piece of information possible **without** external support from the people around you, technology, or an environment that is better designed to suit your needs, is **incorrect**. It has been shaped by systems of oppression such as White supremacy, as well as our capitalist society, and we need to replace it with a new understanding that supporting ourselves and the people around us is not only absolutely okay – but absolutely necessary.

- The more of our brain's capacity we're using up on things like masking, auditory processing, and reminding ourselves of all the different things we need to keep track of, the less capacity we have left to actually work on, keep track of, and remember the things we really need to. If we can find environments where we're safe to unmask and we're better accommodated and supported, our working memory will not feel as impacted or disabling.

- Getting some of the things we're trying to store in our brains down on paper rather than having them buzzing around in our heads every moment of every day, whether that's ideas, to-do's, or the whereabouts of certain objects, can help to reduce some of the strain we put on our working memory.

2

Self-monitoring

I often feel as though, if anything, I am **too** self-aware. After a lifetime of seemingly getting things 'wrong' (whether that's not laughing when a joke has been made, saying the 'wrong' thing at the 'wrong' time, or misunderstanding someone's intentions), without ever really knowing **why,** it has become second nature for me to constantly double, triple, or even quadruple check my thoughts, words or actions before I share them with the world, in the hope of avoiding any more wrongdoing. However, in reality, this is a learned (or perhaps even trauma) response, and my autistic and ADHD brain's natural state is to struggle with **self-monitoring**.

Self-monitoring is defined as the ability to observe and evaluate your own thoughts, behaviours and actions, and explains the ways that we all pay attention to what's going on internally. Like all the other executive functioning skills we'll work through in this book, some aspects of self-monitoring are vital to keeping us safe and well. Thinking right back to our cave-person days, it was important then that we knew we were behaving in a way that would keep us safe from external dangers, and also in favour within our tribe. However, in our modern-day lives, we have become expected to monitor ourselves to incredibly high standards, and it's arguable that some of these expectations, which we'll explore later on in the chapter, would be better left behind.

In this chapter, we will explore:

- **What is self-monitoring?**

- **Which systems have affected the way we think about self-monitoring?**

- **How can we support ourselves with self-monitoring?**

- **5 things to consider putting in place to help with self-monitoring.**

Growing up as an undiagnosed or unsupported neurodivergent person can mean spending a lifetime being misunderstood, questioned and gaslit, which, of course, will have an impact on your ability to notice and trust your own judgements, thoughts and feelings.

Allowing ourselves to make or ask for teeny, tiny adjustments can make a huge difference to the way we feel, or the ways we're able to work, process, and do things.

What is self-monitoring?

Our second executive functioning skill, **self-monitoring**, is defined as the ability to observe and evaluate our own thoughts, behaviours and actions. It describes the process of paying attention to our internal thoughts and processes, as well as our outwardly showing behaviours, and keeping track of what is and isn't working for us. Our brains systematically keep track of what we are doing to improve our practices and our productivity levels, and aim to use this information in order to have increasingly better outcomes. This process of self-monitoring can be split into **two main categories**:

1. **Self-observation**
   This refers to the process of **observing** our thoughts, behaviours and actions, for example, noticing the way that you have behaved in a certain situation.

2. **Self-recording**
   This refers to the process of **recording** our thoughts, behaviours and actions – whether that is physically or mentally. An example of this could be journalling, to record the ways that certain things have made you feel, or keeping a mental note.

Self-monitoring might look like checking in with yourself and asking questions like, 'How do I feel?', 'How is this task going?' or 'Am I on task?' – and either observing the answers to those questions mentally or recording them in some way to use that information going forward.

There are a few key traits of different neurodivergences which might affect our ability to self-monitor as neurodivergent folks:

- **Interoception**
  Autistic people, especially, can struggle with interoception issues. Although we're usually taught that we all have five senses (touch, taste, sight, hearing and smell), in reality there are a couple of extra senses that we all have that are particularly impacted in neurodivergent people. One of those is proprioception (the ability to understand where our body is in space), and another is **interoception**, which I believe really comes into play here. Interoception is defined as **the ability to know and understand what is happening within our bodies.** Autistic people, especially, can struggle with interoception and be either under- or over-sensitive to any sensations. This can show up in ways like:

  – Struggling to know if we are hungry or thirsty.

  – Struggling to know if we need the toilet until the very last minute.

  – Being either under- or over-sensitive to pain.

  – Struggling to explain what pain or sensations in our body feel like.

– Struggling to understand how hot or cold we are.

– Struggling to know which 'feelings' or 'sensations' in our body relate to which emotions.

– Struggling to work out how we are feeling in general.

– Struggling to identify if we are feeling unwell until things become very severe.

– Being either under- or over-sensitive to sensations in our body, such as our heart rate.

If we naturally struggle to interpret our bodies' sensations, or we aren't receiving signals in the same way about what feelings we're having or what things our bodies need, this, obviously, makes it much more tricky to monitor our thoughts, feelings or behaviours. We might **try** to ask ourselves how we're feeling but, in reality, we struggle to be able to work that out.

• **Delayed processing**
Many autistic people report struggling with delayed processing, which means that it can often take us longer than the average person to be able to process what we think or how we feel about something that has happened or something that somebody has said to us. In her book *Safeguarding Autistic Girls*, **Carly Jones MBE** (she/her) describes this as 'where an event occurs, but we [autistic people] don't process and/or display our emotional reaction to that event, be it happy or sad, at the time, instead we do so sometime after'. If we don't immediately process our feelings, and

they instead show up some time after the event, it can be hard to monitor where those feelings come from.

- **Impulsivity**

Neurodivergent people, especially ADHDers, might be prone to experiencing varying levels of impulsivity. We'll dig into this more in the next chapter, **Inhibition/ impulse control (page 133)**, but I think this definitely ties into our ability to self-monitor, too. Examples of impulsivity laid out in the diagnostic criteria for ADHD include:

— Often leaves seat in situations when remaining seated is expected.

— Often runs about or climbs in situations where it is not appropriate (adolescents or adults may be limited to feeling restless).

— Is often 'on the go', acting as if 'driven by a motor'.

— Often talks excessively.

— Often blurts out an answer before a question has been completed.

— Often has trouble waiting their turn.

— Often interrupts or intrudes on others (e.g. butts into conversations or games).

Impulsive action can be broadly defined as the inability to withhold from making a response to a stimulus; if we're always diving right into things, this can make it difficult for us to have the time to stop and think about our thoughts, processes or behaviours.

- **Differences in reading social cues**
Part of the diagnostic criteria for autism is having differences in non-verbal communicative behaviours used for social interaction. This means that we might struggle to understand and use non-verbal communication, such as gestures, facial expressions and eye contact, according to neurotypical norms, for example:

– Struggling to understand and interpret what different facial expressions mean.

– Struggling to understand and interpret the body language of those around us.

– Missing subtle non-verbal context within conversations, such as a change in tone.

– Struggling to 'read between the lines'.

We can also be very literal thinkers and processors, and so we might take things that we are told at face value, or struggle to understand something to be true if it is not communicated to us clearly and directly.

Without being able to understand and interpret all these hidden signals that the people around us are giving out, we are missing vital information about the way that our words, behaviours and actions are received or perceived by other people. Knowing if something has been taken 'well' or interpreted 'badly' is vital feedback for us to be able to self-monitor and work out if these are behaviours that we should continue to use in the future, or if they are behaviours that we might want to change or improve in some way.

Which systems have affected the way we think about self-monitoring?

As with all the executive functions we will explore throughout the book, although the ability to monitor our own thoughts, actions and behaviour is a vital skill for us to have, the ways in which we currently consider 'deficits' in self-monitoring are socially constructed and impacted by different biases within our society.

I think it's really important that we start off here by discussing **ableism** and the ways it forces us to monitor our behaviours on a constant basis. In our society, we have been led to believe that any divergence from the norm is 'wrong' or 'bad'. This shows up in ableism, which means that we look down on or negatively judge disabled people or the traits that they have as a result of their disability. As an example, throughout the diagnostic criteria for autism, ADHD, and most other neurodivergences, the traits or experiences of neurodivergent people are framed as 'deficits'. We are told we have 'deficits' in social abilities, 'deficits' in communication, 'deficits' in our ability to focus, or 'deficits' in our ability to develop relationships. In fact, none of these things are actually deficits – they are just **differences**. I discuss this more thoroughly throughout my first book, ***unmasked***, as well as the ways that we are forced to **mask** our differences in order to be safe and accepted in society.

Masking is the act of hiding or disguising parts of ourselves in order to better fit in with the people around us. It explains the way that an autistic (or otherwise neurodivergent) person attempts to appear non-autistic (or neurotypical) by covering up their autistic (or neurodivergent) traits. It was initially and is most commonly used to explain specifically the autistic experience, but more recently, it has also been adopted and used by the neurodivergent community as a whole. As **Dr Hannah Belcher** (she/her) explains in an article for the National Autistic Society: 'Masking may involve suppressing certain behaviours we find soothing but that others think are "weird", such as stimming or intense interests. It can also mean mimicking the behaviour of those around us, such as copying non-verbal behaviours, and developing complex social scripts to get by in social situations.'

It might look like:

- **Camouflaging:** Covering up or obscuring neurodivergent traits, tendencies or characteristics in order to 'blend in' to a neurotypical social environment.

- **Mimicking:** Copying the behaviours of those around you.

- **Over-compensating:** Actively counterbalancing your natural traits/behaviours by using specific strategies to maintain the appearance of functioning in the same way as everyone else.

In the context of self-monitoring, I think it's really important that we consider just how much **extra** self-monitoring we are expected to do as neurodivergent people in order to fit into our society. Where other people might just go about their lives, not really having to question too many of their natural behaviours or ways of being, we are constantly monitoring:

- Whether we are making too much or too little eye contact.

- Whether we are doing a good enough job of suppressing our stims.

- Whether we are making the right facial expressions at the right time.

- Whether we are showing enough signs that we are interested in the conversation, for example, by nodding or making encouraging noises.

- Whether we are using a friendly enough tone of voice – rather than our natural one, which might be more blunt and monotonous and therefore perceived as rude.

- Whether we are talking too much about our special interests and therefore risking being told that we are annoying or self-centred.

Instead of us having a 'deficit' in self-monitoring, I'd actually argue that we could probably all be self-monitoring gold-medal-winning Olympic champions! The reality might not be that we struggle to self-monitor; it might be that we're expected (or forced) to monitor so many **more** aspects of ourselves than any neurotypical person is expected to, and so, naturally, sometimes there are going to be a couple of behaviours that slip through the cracks. Additionally, allowing these behaviours to slip through the cracks (and, therefore, unmasking) should not be seen as a negative thing, a 'deficit', or something that needs to be worked on; it should be **actively encouraged**!

In addition to ableism, I also think our patriarchal society and the misogyny within it have huge implications for the ways that women and people marginalized for their gender are required to self-monitor. As Gina Martin shared in **What defines our view of executive functioning? (page 19)**, 'Girls are socialised to be agreeable, small and facilitating – which is a masking of its own kind – and that plays heavily into how well they learn to mask their neurodivergence at such an early age.'

Presenting in these polite, quiet and controlled ways requires a huge amount of self-observation and monitoring. This becomes twofold for women and people marginalized for their gender whose intersecting identities mean that they are marginalized by multiple systems of oppression, for example, queer women, trans women and people marginalized for their gender, and women of colour.

We are even forced to self-monitor simply to keep ourselves safe. As **Ellen Jones** (she/her), queer and autistic author, speaker and creator, explains:

The world demands that women and other marginalized people be hypervigilant at all times. Our safety is often contingent not just

on the ability to recognize potential threats –
men following us on the way home, controlling
behaviours, exploitation by a boss – but also on
the ways we might be able to attempt to mitigate
them. We are often taught that there are things
we might have done differently and blamed for
the outcomes. The truth is that no amount of
self-monitoring can prevent discrimination. We
try – as some thinly veiled harm reduction – but
it doesn't work. My experience is that autistic
women tend to swing wildly between extreme
hypervigilance and obliviousness, the latter often
being a compensatory behaviour to the former. The
responsibility shouldn't be on us, but it is.

Demi Colleen (she/her), Black and neurodivergent content creator
and writer, adds:

Self-monitoring becomes a more complex tool
when race is a factor. As a Black woman with
ADHD, cultural influence and outside perception
can make reflecting on one's behaviour a confusing
task. I found this particularly difficult when adjusting
my behaviours in school and social situations. In
an educational setting, I experienced prejudice
from the teachers and would be unfairly punished
for exhibiting the same behaviours as my white
classmates. Though I was mirroring their behaviour,
only I would be perceived as a troublemaker. It felt

impossible to monitor my behaviours effectively when the results and impact were so inconsistent, and I couldn't understand why at the time. The playing field was never equal, so the goalpost changed frequently.

Following on from this, there are also aspects of White supremacy culture, outlined in Tema Okun's characteristics (more on this in **What defines our view of executive functioning?, page 19**), which impact our views on self-monitoring. One of these characteristics is **qualified**, which explains the way that White people, or those from dominant groups, are inclined to feel inherently more qualified, entitled or equipped than non-White or marginalized people. They might assume their own inherent qualification to 'fix' whatever is in front of them that is 'broken' (read, different) without acknowledging their role in breaking it – or that it might not be broken at all.

This characteristic is similar to **One Right Way** (which we explored in **What defines our view of executive functioning?, page 19**) and explains someone's own bias towards always assuming that they know best. An example of this that many of us will be able to relate to might be when someone (who is not an ADHDer themselves) tells us about their *brilliant* new planner or that we **just** need to set more alarms or write more to-do lists. They automatically assume, thanks to their internal bias of being 'qualified', that they are best placed to tell us how to 'fix' our problems when, in reality, they don't have any of the lived experience to be able to do that.

Some examples of the ways the 'qualified' characteristic affects the way we see executive functioning and self-monitoring:

- Those without lived experience of neurodivergence often consider themselves to be experts on neurodivergence, regardless of their lack of personal understanding. This might mean that they assume we are 'lacking in self-monitoring' when, in reality, we just have different ways of working, thinking and behaving, and so will naturally monitor ourselves in different ways.

- Those without lived experience of neurodivergence might define the ways that we 'should' self-monitor, work or function differently from their own lack of personal experience, which can cause miscommunication or misunderstandings, particularly in the workplace.

- Those who hold power may not consider how their behaviour or expectations might be negatively impacting neurodivergent people – for example, that it could be the working conditions (tight deadlines, being understaffed, or having unclear expectations) which cause someone to struggle. They therefore incorrectly blame any difficulties on the neurodivergent person's ability to self-monitor or self-manage.

This context and understanding might be helpful to carry forward while we look at ways we can support ourselves with self-monitoring, especially when it comes to masking. Instead of carefully monitoring and controlling our every move, which would be unhelpful, harmful and draining, we can reframe the idea of self-monitoring into something more like **self-knowing**. It's not about thinking, 'These are my natural ways of being, and they are "wrong" so I need to monitor and change them,' but instead, 'I have been able to notice that my brain works in these ways, so what can I do to lean into those natural ways of being to make life easier and better for myself?'

Self-awareness, or self-monitoring, can be an incredibly useful skill if we approach it with **compassion** rather than attempting to 'fix' things. The aim is to look at our differences, strengths, struggles and weaknesses through a neutral lens and think, 'This is the way that things tend to flow for me, so how can I go with the current, rather than constantly trying to either swim upstream or build a dam to stop the flow altogether?'

The tips over the following pages are designed to help you get more in tune with the way you self-monitor and, therefore, find ways of working with your brain rather than against it. But it's equally important (as people who are likely to have spent a lot of our lives monitoring our every thought, word and action) that we don't get too caught up in monitoring ourselves to the point that we're masking, criticizing and shaming. We're aiming to find a balance between letting go of the neuronormative 'shoulds' that don't serve us, and picking up tips and tricks that can support us in making the ones that we need to follow work better for us.

How can we support ourselves with self-monitoring?

Similarly to our **working memory**, which we explored in the previous chapter, being better supported with self-monitoring isn't completely reliant on us as individuals, but instead equally relies on us being supported and accommodated by the people around us and the environments that we enter. As we touched on previously, masking requires a consistent and significant level of self-observation and self-monitoring. As **Dr Hannah Louise Belcher** (she/her) explains in her book *Taking Off the Mask*:

> We can't mimic others' behaviour unless we have the ability to remember the behaviour we have seen. We can't apply our learned social scripts to new situations without the ability to plan ahead and be flexible to new situations and changes.

This puts a huge strain on our executive functioning capabilities and, therefore, takes away from our capacity to monitor the things that will *actually* help us. It also perhaps explains why masking or camouflaging is so exhausting for autistic and otherwise neurodivergent people: we are constantly using a strategy which requires a huge amount of executive functioning, when our executive functioning capabilities are thought to be delayed or limited to begin with!

If we have spent our entire lives doing all the background work that masking consists of, and being in a near-enough constant state of fight or flight, we haven't been able to stop and think, 'How am I feeling right now?' We have been stuck in survival mode rather than having the capacity to focus on anything other than getting through the current 'danger'. This more helpful sort of self-reflection requires us to be in a **calm and safe environment where we know that we don't need to be on guard in case of any looming danger.** Therefore, if we can find environments where we feel **understood and supported**, and where we know that we are safe to unmask, we can let go of some of the unhelpful self-monitoring (like 'Am I making enough eye contact?' or 'Is my tone of voice animated enough?'), and free up space for more helpful self-monitoring. This helpful self-monitoring might look like asking ourselves how we feel, what we need, what would help us, or what we do and don't like.

Many autistic people, especially those who have spent a considerable amount of time undiagnosed, report experiencing a huge amount of difficulty when trying to work out how they feel or what does and doesn't feel good. They have spent such a long time being told that their needs don't matter, or are wrong, that they've lost the ability to trust their own instinct. As an example, if you are repeatedly told that you are dramatic or attention-seeking for feeling upset or wobbled by things, you learn that your feelings are 'wrong' and, before long, will start to cover them up completely and eventually push them down so far that you don't even recognize the feelings yourself. Growing up as an undiagnosed or unsupported neurodivergent person can mean spending a lifetime being misunderstood, questioned and gaslit, which, of course, will have an impact on your ability to notice and trust your own judgements, thoughts and feelings. If you are repeatedly told and convinced that your perception of events is wrong, your experiences and pain are fictional, and your needs are invalid, you will naturally begin to question your own judgement. Add this to the fact that our differences in interoception can mean that we struggle to identify emotions or sensations in our bodies to begin with, and it's no wonder that trying to work out how we feel can be difficult. As **Carly Jones MBE** (she/her) explains in her book *Safeguarding Autistic Girls*, this can have very dangerous consequences:

> If from childhood an Autistic girl is told, 'The music in the car isn't too loud, you're being silly!' when it actually feels as if her ears are bleeding due to sensory issues, would she be more likely to accept that she makes mistakes when she's told by an abuser that her perceptions are wrong?

With this executive function, I think it's really important to be gentle with yourself and trust that, even if finding this self-awareness or self-monitoring feels difficult initially, over time you will begin to find ways of tuning into your body and your feelings and working these things out. Think of self-monitoring as a muscle which needs to be trained rather than something that you will see changes in overnight. The more that you carve out the time to sit with your feelings and ask yourselves these questions, and the more time that you spend with people and in places where you can begin to unmask and remove yourself from the 'fight or flight' state, the more you will be able to notice how you really feel, and what you really think.

Some of my top suggestions on how to begin to unmask, which you can read more about in my first book, **unmasked**, are as follows:

- **Find ways of listening to your body.** We'll get into this more in the tips on the following pages.

- **Lean into your special interests.** Spending time throwing yourself into the things you love the most can really help you feel safe and most like your true self.

- **Spend time with other neurodivergent people.** What better way to start being more authentic than to surround yourself with people just like you?

- **Spend time alone.** Whenever you are interacting with the outside world, there is going to be an aspect of being aware that you are being perceived, and therefore masking or monitoring yourself in order to try and control that perception and ensure it is a positive one.

Before we get into our main self-monitoring strategies, tips and tricks, like in the last chapter, I want to quickly set the scene by reminding you of a list of things that are **absolutely fine** to do or ask for. Allowing ourselves to make or ask for teeny, tiny adjustments can make a huge difference to the way we feel, or the ways we're able to work, process and do things.

A list of things that are <u>absolutely fine</u>:

- Asking to have some time to consider how you think and feel about a request before saying yes or no.

- Asking to have some time to process how you feel about something somebody has said to you before responding.

- Asking to receive these requests or 'big' or 'important' communications via email or text message rather than verbally or face-to-face, so you have that time to process and consider.

- Spending more time alone to give yourself time to check in with yourself.

- Spending less time socializing with people you have known for a long time and more time socializing with newer neurodivergent friends who you feel you can better unmask around.

- Not making or forcing eye-contact, and instead looking wherever feels most comfortable for you.

- No longer monitoring and suppressing the ways that you might want to stim or self-regulate, and instead freely moving however feels good.

- No longer monitoring or altering your tone of voice, and instead speaking in a way that feels natural to you, even if that might be considered more 'blunt'.

- Speaking freely or info-dumping about your special interests, rather than constantly trying to ensure you haven't spoken about them 'too much'.

- Using tools like the 'Emotion Sensation Feeling Wheel' by Lindsay Braman to help you identify the ways that you feel (see my references at the back of the book).

- Finding ways of journalling, checking in with yourself and processing that suit you, like recording voice notes on your phone as and when you need to, rather than feeling like you have to journal in a written diary for ten minutes every morning, for example.

Tip 6:
The mood for food

By Vanessa D'Souza (she/her), The Autistic Chef™ – MasterChef semi-finalist and content creator

As an AuDHDer with sensory processing difficulties, I am super passionate about making the world of food, cooking and feeding yourself more accessible to other neurodivergent folks. By self-monitoring, we can identify which parts of eating/feeding ourselves feel most difficult for us, and put a variety of things in place to work with our neurodivergent brains, rather than against them.

Below are some of my top tips and practical strategies which can be implemented to help with the challenges that can come with being neurodivergent, to ensure you have a balanced and enjoyable approach to food and feeding yourself.

Autistic individuals

Sensory-friendly mealtimes:

- Use **non-distracting utensils and dishware** to reduce overwhelm.

- Stick to foods with **textures/smells/tastes** which are preferred.

- Have a **comfortable eating environment** specific to that person (i.e. eating alone to avoid being perceived, dim lighting, ear defenders).

Visual schedules for meal prep:

- Having a **visual schedule for meal preparation** can help provide structure and reduce anxiety: this can include using pictures of ingredients rather than words/text, or watching video tutorials rather than reading each stage of the cooking method.

Routine and predictability:

- For those who need routine/structure, **having a consistent mealtime wherever possible** provides a sense of necessary predictability.

Limiting food options:

- Respect and accommodate any food aversions/ preferences – whether that's when cooking for an autistic person, or learning to be more compassionate with yourself.

- Have a limited selection of choices to avoid decision overwhelm.

ADHD individuals

Meal planning and prepping:

- Plan and prep meals **in advance** to reduce decision paralysis.

- Have **pre-prepped ingredients** (like using frozen pre-chopped items) to speed things up and help make things more manageable.

- Use **dopamine serving plates**, or colourful patterns.

Regular snack breaks:

- If you struggle with interoception, **keep snacks close by** throughout the day to maintain energy levels, setting timers to eat them regularly. Same goes for water, as often it's thirst, not hunger (though I still cannot tell the difference myself!).

- It's proven that a mix of **protein and complex carbs** (for example, a meal of chicken with sweet potato fries, or wholemeal pasta with mince bolognese) can help sustain attention and focus.

Visual reminders:

- Incorporate visual timers or alarms to signal when it's time to start preparing or eating.

- Use visual step-by-step guides to keep you on track during the cooking or preparation process.

- This can help ensure things don't get forgotten about, especially when cooking, or the impatience of taking things out before they are cooked.

General tips which work for me:

No-cooking cooking:

- Keeping healthy freezer-ready meals for executive dysfunction days, and dry packet meals (like instant noodles), microwave steam veggie bags and microwave rice for the days when you have little/no energy but want to eat well.

- If you can afford it, choosing a meal delivery kit option (such as HelloFresh, Gousto, or Mindful Chef) can both take away decision paralysis and mean you get a nutritious meal. I always choose things that can be made quickly, and it also means I don't need to do a big food shop, and there is no waste.

For those with dyspraxia/dyscalculia/or those who struggle with fine motor skills:

- Always buy pre-cut/peeled/pre-made items — I love frozen chopped onions, frozen minced garlic, cut and washed veggies, which mean I don't need to do as much work.

- Use cups as a metric instead of weighing in grams if you follow a recipe — this can be easier if you struggle with numbers.

Tip 7:
Honouring your sensory needs

Before I knew I was an autistic ADHDer, I used to experience really intense bouts of burnout every six months, like clockwork. I would become incredibly overwhelmed, tired, tearful, and really struggle with my mental health. No matter how hard I tried to avoid these periods of burnout and low mood (for example, by eating well, exercising, going to therapy and taking anti-depressants), they would always catch up with me.

Looking back, I now know that (as well as being caused by the huge amounts of masking I was doing without ever realizing) this burnout was the result of not having a vital piece of information about the way that my brain worked. I didn't know that I was neurodivergent, and so I was missing one really key thing from my routine.

Now I know that I'm an autistic ADHDer and have spent time exploring what that means, I know that I need to schedule time into my routine to **honour my sensory needs**.

Despite autism historically being framed as a mostly social and communication disability, many autistic people argue that the biggest difference in their experience is in the ways that they process sensory input. We can be **over- or under-sensitive** to:

- **Light:** for example, struggling with bright, fluorescent lighting, such as in a supermarket or airport, or enjoying flashing lights like fairy lights or starlight projectors.

- **Sound:** for example, becoming overwhelmed if there are different clashing sounds, like somebody talking while the TV is on, or seeking out loud sounds by playing music very loudly in your headphones.

- **Smell:** for example, feeling distracted if there is a different smell in your environment (I couldn't possibly let this moment pass without using the example of my brother, Lewis, hating cheese and onion crisps more than **anything** on this earth and having to move seats – or even carriages – on public transport if someone was to open a packet), or enjoying seeking out different scents, like having a very strong signature perfume.

- **Texture:** for example, not liking unusual textures of food (I personally hate fish and seafood because of the slimy texture) or seeking out different textures like really crunchy crisps.

- **Touch or pressure:** for example, feeling uncomfortable when clothes or labels are touching your skin, or seeking out pressure in the form of a deep-tissue massage.

Since we can be either over- or under-sensitive to each type of sensory input – and, often, a combination of the two at different times or in different situations – it's really important that we make time to honour our sensory needs with both **sensory-avoiding** behaviours (where we're limiting the sensory input we need to process) and **sensory-seeking** behaviours (where we're seeking out extra or increased sensory input).

Over the following pages are some examples of sensory-seeking and sensory-avoiding behaviours for each of the senses explored above, with space for you to add some examples of your own. I would also highly recommend that, instead of just hoping that you get around to implementing these things (which, especially if you are an ADHDer like me, seems unlikely), you schedule a regular slot in your diary or calendar for sensory-seeking or sensory-avoiding time. This is a really good chance to practise a bit of self-monitoring by checking in with yourself and working out which senses you need to avoid or seek out at that current time, which will change depending on how you're feeling or the day that you've had. For example, if you have spent the day in a busy office with lots of overlapping sounds and bright light, you will probably want to spend some time avoiding lights and sounds by lying in a quiet, dark room – or maybe listening to some white noise.

Sensory input	Sensory-avoiding behaviours	Sensory-seeking behaviours
Light	– Lying in a dark room – Using soft lamplight rather than the 'big' light – _____ – _____ – _____	– Filling your space with visual stims, for example a liquid motion bubbler – Watching a starlight projector or twinkling fairy lights – _____ – _____ – _____
Sound	– Wearing noise-cancelling headphones or ear defenders – Lying in a quiet room – _____ – _____ – _____	– Listening to white, pink or brown noise to help you get off to sleep – Listening to a podcast or video in the background while you work – _____ – _____ – _____
Smell	– Buying scentless candles or laundry detergent – Keeping things like flowers out of your bedroom – _____ – _____ – _____	– Wearing a strong signature scent – Cooking fresh food or using fresh herbs and spices – _____ – _____ – _____

Sensory input	Sensory-avoiding behaviours	Sensory-seeking behaviours
Texture	– Avoiding certain textures of food – Wearing washing-up gloves to avoid the texture of food in the sink – _____ – _____ – _____	– Seeking out textures of food like crunchy food – Playing with sand or slime – _____ – _____ – _____
Touch or pressure	– Wearing one of our (un)masked 'I'm a no touch type of person' pin badges so that people don't hug you at events or family gatherings – Wearing baggy clothes so they don't touch your skin as much – _____ – _____ – _____	– Having a deep-pressure massage – Lying under a weighted blanket – _____ – _____ – _____

Tip 8:
Avoiding demand avoidance

One of my biggest self-monitoring discoveries since finding out that I am neurodivergent has been how significantly I am impacted by **demand avoidance**. Demand avoidance is something that many autistic people, especially, experience, and describes the way that our brains will be incredibly resistant to anything that we perceive to be a demand. This demand, whether real or perceived, might be an expectation, a request, or some other kind of external 'pressure', and, when picked up by our brains, can activate our nervous system, send us into a state of fight or flight, and lead us to avoid the 'demand' at all costs.

Pathological Demand Avoidance (or PDA) was previously considered to be a unique profile of autism. However, more recently, the community have begun to reframe PDA as standing for a **Persistent Drive for Autonomy**, as this feels more neurodivergence-affirming than something being 'pathological', as well as more accurate in terms of our internal experience rather than viewing it from an outsider's perspective. We have also started to see demand avoidance as being another trait or experience that falls within the autism spectrum, which different autistic people experience to a greater or lesser degree, rather than being a separate 'profile'.

Demand avoidance, or drive for autonomy, is something that has a huge impact on the way that I am able to live, work and behave. One example that you might find easy to relate to (whether you are an autistic person or not) is when you are just about to empty the dishwasher, and somebody says, 'Oh, please could you empty the dishwasher?' or even, 'Oh, the dishwasher needs emptying!' Suddenly, even though you were literally **just** about to start the task at hand, you might feel a really strong resistance to actually going on to do it. This is the case for so many aspects of my life, all the way from struggling to complete actual demands, like instructions, through to seemingly silly things like not being able to watch popular films when they are first released because the 'buzz' or 'hype' around them feels like a demand that I 'should' watch it, and so my demand avoidance immediately feels like it has lost some sort of autonomy and resists watching it.

After **self-monitoring** and figuring out that I experience demand avoidance, I'm able to work with my brain (instead of against it) by removing demands from my life wherever possible. By doing this, I'm lessening the amount of times that my nervous system is triggered into resisting certain tasks, and therefore I am more likely to be able to get them done. Below is a list of some of the ways that I have put this into practice, with some space for you to reflect on your own examples of 'demands' that you could reduce or replace.

Ways I could reduce or reframe demands:

- Instead of having a set posting schedule for my social media accounts — for example, that I must post a quote every Monday, a video every Tuesday, and so on — I just allow myself to post as and when I feel like it.

- Instead of scheduling certain tasks in my calendar for a certain date and time in advance (which then feels like a demand to complete them at that time), I will put them on my to-do list for the week and then pick out the tasks that I am going to complete each day.

- Instead of making a meal plan for the week (which then feels like a demand to cook or eat that meal on that day), you could make a list of the meals that you will eat throughout the week, buy the ingredients, and then allow yourself to choose which meal you fancy on the day.

- _____
  _____
  _____

- _____
  _____
  _____

- _____
  _____
  _____

- _____
  _____
  _____

Tip 9:
Safe word

Something else that you might notice once you begin to practise self-monitoring and get more in tune with how you feel is that there are times when you become very overwhelmed, for example, experiencing autistic meltdowns or shutdowns. You might even find that these become more frequent as you begin to unmask and spend less time covering up the way that you feel.

During both autistic meltdowns and autistic shutdowns (or other intense periods of overwhelm like anxiety attacks or just stressful situations in general), you will most likely find it difficult to communicate with the people around you. This might be losing the ability to use your words completely and experiencing a verbal shutdown, or it might just be that while your brain is so overwhelmed, it's difficult to piece together the words you need to form sentences that are coherent or make sense to the people around you.

These situations are not fun (understatement of the century), but one thing that I've found which can make them slightly more bearable is to have a pre-agreed **safe word** or **code word** with someone you feel comfortable with, so that, even when communication becomes difficult or impossible, you can still communicate what you need to.

This could look like agreeing with your partner that you will say, 'We need to get back to the car before the parking runs out' if you need to leave a social situation, so that you can communicate the fact you need to leave without having to explain that you're struggling. Your partner would then know not to question or try to convince you to stay and that, by saying that, you were signalling that you needed to get out of there with as little friction as possible. Another example could be that you agree with your manager that you will say, 'I'm just going to collect something from the printer,' if you need to leave a meeting or a loud office so that you can communicate that you need to go and take some quiet time to decompress, without feeling like you need to explain or justify in front of your colleagues.

If verbal communication is particularly difficult for you, you could even use physical gestures (like saying that you will tap your partner three times on their right arm if you need their help) or use **communication cards** or **AAC (Augmentative and Alternative Communication) devices** to communicate non-verbally. It doesn't matter what code word or signal you use (it could be a completely random word or phrase that nobody else in the room would understand!); what matters is that it's pre-arranged between you and your safe person to **relieve the need to communicate or express yourself in the moment**.

Below are some prompts to help you to work out what situations it might be helpful to have a safe word in, who your safe person or contact might be in that situation, and what word or phrase you could agree to use.

Potentially stressful situation	Who is my safe person?	What could my safe word/phrase/gesture be?

Tip 10:
Interoception check-in

By Beaux Miebach (they/them), inclusion & belonging lead at Tiimo

I'm one of those people who can easily go about their day getting few (or no) signals from my body to drink water, eat or rest. I used to end my days feeling cranky, headache-y and upset, with no real understanding of why and how to feel better.

Exploring my neurodivergence meant learning a **whole lot more** about how and why I function the way I do, and when I finally learned about interoception, I felt like years of unexplained headaches finally made sense.

Interoception, or the signals our body gives us to tell us if we're thirsty, hungry or in pain, is an important part of sensory processing that, as with many other things, can often look different for neurodivergent folks. I have what is called an under-responsive system, which means that I often don't respond to sensory inputs until they are really strong (for example, I may not realize I'm thirsty until I'm *super* thirsty), but there are other kinds of interoception differences including over-responsivity (feeling sensations more intensely or for longer), and having discrimination difficulties (trouble telling how you feel or what you need).

As with most things, there is no one 'right' way to experience sensory inputs, but where it gets tricky is if the way your body experiences sensations affects your ability to self-regulate or puts you at risk of serious harm (e.g. you don't feel pain until it's excruciating). Because, in the past, my under-responsivity affected how I could show up for myself and my community, I started exploring ways to work with my system and found that the best way to meet my needs is to set **interoception check-in reminders**!

I use **Tiimo**, a neuroinclusive planning app, to remind myself to check in with my nervous system. My **three daily reminders** guide me through a series of questions that help me tune into my body and meet any unmet needs, like, for example, going to the bathroom. For folks who are over-reactive, these interoception check-ins can help you ground and ensure you're meeting your needs at consistent intervals. For example, if you know that you need around eight cups of water a day, you can schedule four check-ins daily to make sure you've had two cups of water since your last check-in. People with sensory-discrimination difficulties can also benefit from this method and use these check-ins as an intentional time to sit with their bodies and tune into what they need.

This method has helped me (and my pals along the spectrum of sensory processing differences) be proactive about self-care and has made for happier, more grounded days. Give it a try!

Monday

M	T	W	T	F	S	M
9	10	11	12	13	14	15
16	17	18	19	20	21	22

Cancel   Save

Interoception Check-in

Time to make sure your needs are met!

Time 15:00 – 15:10 (10 minutes)

Every day

✓ **Create checklist**

⬛ Have you drunk enough water today?

⬛ When was the last time you ate?

⬛ Have you been to the toilet?

⬛ Have you brushed your teeth?

⬛ How are you feeling emotionally?

⬛ Does anything hurt?

➕ Add new task

—

Self-monitoring recap

Our second executive function, **self-monitoring**, is defined as the extent to which someone monitors their self-presentations, expressive behaviour and non-verbal affective displays. It describes the ways that we observe and evaluate our own thoughts, behaviours and actions, and the ways that we all pay attention to what's going on internally. This skill is important in making sure we act in ways that are safe, productive and well-received, but can lead to us over-monitoring our behaviours, such as when masking.

In this chapter, we have explored:

- What self-monitoring is.

- The systems which have affected the way we think about self-monitoring.

- Some ways we can support ourselves with self-monitoring.

- 5 things to consider putting in place for self-monitoring.

Your takeaway box

- As neurodivergent people, we are often self-monitoring to a really high degree, asking ourselves questions like 'Am I making enough eye contact?' or 'Am I nodding enough and making the right noises to

---

appear interested?' This can be more unhelpful than it is productive, and takes away from our capacity to monitor what's really important, such as how we feel.

- Our ability to self-monitor can also be impacted by growing up undiagnosed or unsupported in a neurotypical world. If you are repeatedly told and convinced that your perception of events is wrong, your experiences and pain are fictional, and your needs are invalid, you will naturally begin to question your own judgement. Know that it is only natural that your ability to self-monitor would be impacted, but that, over time and with practice, you can get back to trusting and listening to yourself.

- Scheduling time into our diaries to check in with ourselves and make sure that we're getting our needs met can be a helpful way to bring self-monitoring back into our consciousness. The more you practise, the more you will naturally begin to notice.

3

Inhibition/impulse control

As someone who is covered in over fifty tattoos (most of which weren't booked ahead of time), who has dyed her hair almost every colour possible, and who travelled the world for two years on one month's notice, I perhaps should have realized that my impulse control was slightly 'off' sooner than I did. I have always whirred through life at a hundred miles per hour – rarely taking the time to stop and consider my options, but instead rushing full steam ahead into any decision, no matter how important.

Before my ADHD diagnosis, I booked holidays without considering whether I could actually get the time off work, applied for jobs without taking the time to think about whether it was something I *actually* wanted to do, and booked whatever tickets I could get my hands on to go and see my favourite bands live in concert, even if the gig was at the other side of the country and I had no idea how I might get there or who might be interested in coming with me. Looking back, I now know that this is because **inhibition/impulse control** is one of the executive functioning skills that is impacted in neurodivergent brains.

In this chapter, we will explore:

- What is inhibition/impulse control?

- Which systems have affected the way we think about inhibition/impulse control?

- How can we support ourselves with inhibition/impulse control?

- 5 things to consider putting in place for your inhibition/impulse control.

Our brains don't stop us jumping into things in the same way that other people's do, so we have to find ways of manually putting some sort of barrier into place to hold us back from going full steam ahead.

Asking people to
tweak the ways
in which they
communicate with you
to better support your
brain is not too much
to ask.

What is inhibition/impulse control?

Our next executive functioning skill, **inhibition/impulse control**, is defined as the ability to resist impulsive urges and hold back from inappropriate or disruptive behaviours. Put simply, it describes our brain's ability to stop and think about whether something is a good idea, rather than jumping straight in. This skill is frequently impacted in neurodivergent people – especially for ADHDers, where impulsivity makes up a big part of the diagnostic criteria.

The DSM-5 is the fifth edition of the *Diagnostic and Statistical Manual of Mental Disorders*, which is frequently used to assess and medically diagnose many neurodivergences, including ADHD. It includes the following examples of impulsive behaviour, which make up part of the diagnostic criteria for ADHD:

- Often leaves seat in situations when remaining seated is expected.

- Often runs about or climbs in situations where it is not appropriate (adolescents or adults may be limited to feeling restless).

- Is often 'on the go', acting as if 'driven by a motor'.

- Often talks excessively.

- Often blurts out an answer before a question has been completed.

- Often has trouble waiting their turn.

- Often interrupts or intrudes on others (e.g. butts into conversations or games).

These impulsive behaviours, as is the case for much of the diagnostic criteria, appear to focus more on examples of impulsivity that are visibly obvious to the people around us rather than our own internal experiences. They also seem to describe experiences that might be more common in children, that teenagers or adults may have learned to mask throughout their lives. Other less obvious, more internal, or less easily masked examples of impulsive behaviour might include:

- Spending money without considering the consequences.

- Saying something without considering if it might be hurtful or inappropriate.

- Booking holidays without considering if you're actually able to go.

- Quitting your job on a whim.

- Finding it hard to resist risky, self-destructive behaviours, for example, unsafe sex or bingeing on drugs or alcohol.

- Binge-eating or eating to the point that you feel sick.

- Becoming suddenly angry at the flick of a switch.

- Feeling physical discomfort when having to wait in line.

- Jumping straight into tasks without planning first.

- Having racing thoughts that are hard to control.

- Spur-of-the-moment decision-making, even when it is a big or important decision.

Researchers have suggested a couple of reasons that we might struggle with inhibition/impulse control. The first is that it could be associated with an **imbalance of neurotransmitters in the brain**.

Explained simply, the human brain uses a combination of hormones to make decisions about what we should or should not do, including 'happy' hormones, which reinforce behaviours that make us feel good to encourage us to repeat them. When it comes to impulse control, it has been suggested that two of these hormones in particular, **dopamine and serotonin**, are at play. Dopamine is described as the brain's 'go' signal – it motivates us to get going (or keep going) with an activity that needs to be done, and serotonin is described as the 'no go' signal, which lets us know that we're content, we have done enough, and it's okay to stop and enjoy the feeling.

In a neurotypical brain, it's thought that the balance between the two is pretty stable, and so somebody will get just enough of the motivational dopamine to get them going, followed by just enough serotonin to let them know that it's okay to stop. In certain situations, the 'go' dopamine will increase and motivate them to indulge in an impulse (like when it's important to make a quick decision and get going), and, at other times, the 'no go' serotonin levels will override the dopamine and stop them acting impulsively – working together as the inhibition/impulse control.

Whereas, it has been suggested that when somebody has ADHD (and this could perhaps be the case for other neurodivergent folks, too), they have a lower number of dopamine receptors in the brain. This means that, during ordinary tasks, we might receive fewer of the 'go' signals – which explains why we can struggle with other executive functioning skills like task initiation.

So, how does this link to impulsivity? Well, one study suggested that since we *usually* have lower levels of dopamine, when we *do* get a dopamine hit, it triggers an **even higher amount of dopamine in our usually-dopamine-deficient brains**, meaning it completely overrides the levels of serotonin and makes us more likely to act impulsively.

Research in this area is very limited, and many people feel that the 'dopamine' explanation of ADHD oversimplifies what is really going on, but this theory goes some way to explaining why it is that we might struggle to control our impulses in the same ways that other people can.

Which systems have affected the way we think about inhibition/impulse control?

As with all executive functioning skills, we do need to be able to control our impulses to a certain level. Impulsive behaviour in ADHDers, especially, can lead to dangerous and difficult experiences, including the examples below which I shared in my first book, *unmasked*:

- Adults with ADHD are nine times more likely to end up in prison than those of a similar age and background who do not have ADHD.

- Adults with ADHD are far more likely than those without to engage in risky financial behaviour, such as taking out expensive loans or making impulsive purchases without thinking the implications through fully. 60% of ADHDers said that it directly impacts their financial lives because of issues with money management, costing them, on average, an estimated £1,600 per year.

- According to a study conducted at Harvard Medical School in 2007, girls with ADHD were almost four times more likely to have an eating disorder than those without ADHD.

So, of course, it is important that we are supported to find ways of improving our impulse control. However, I believe that, as with all the executive functioning skills that we will explore throughout the book, the way that we currently think about impulsivity has been defined by some of the biases that show up in our society.

One place to start is with ableism. As mentioned above, the examples of impulsivity given in the diagnostic criteria for ADHD are mostly through the lens of somebody else's view of an ADHDer, rather than the experiences of the ADHDer themselves. They describe behaviours that are seen as 'annoying', 'disruptive' or 'inconsiderate' by society, when, much of the time, there is no actual reason for this; it is simply that we've been taught, over time, that this is the way we should see these behaviours. For example:

- **Often leaves seat in situations when remaining seated is expected.**
  Who decided that we have to sit down for long periods of time and it is 'bad' to prefer to stand or move around? Why is it impulsive to stand up and walk around during a meeting, rather than being seen as a perfectly normal thing that a human might choose to do. Research has actually shown that the act of walking leads to an increase in creative thinking, which suggests that walking meetings might actually improve our ways of working and ability to problem-solve.

- **Often talks excessively.**
  Who decides what is a normal vs 'excessive' amount to talk? Surely this is dependent on circumstance, mood and personal preference, rather than a clearly defined amount? We have been conditioned to think it is 'rude' for people to speak a lot or over other people in conversation, when, in reality, we should be more aware of **why** someone might be doing that and accept that that's someone's natural communication style – otherwise it's *us* that is actually being rude to that person!

- **Often blurts out an answer before a question has been completed.**

Why did we decide that being able to answer a question quickly was a bad thing? Sure, waiting gives other people the chance to work it out in a classroom environment, for example. But surely answering a question quickly is actually a good thing, because it shows that a) you are listening and b) you have the knowledge required to provide an answer or solution?

- **Often has trouble waiting their turn.**

Perhaps if we hadn't created a society that involves so much queuing and waiting, then having trouble waiting your turn would not be such a disabling trait? A lot of the times that we have to queue and wait are because of our consumerism and capitalist society, for example waiting to get to the counter in a shop, or because of services that don't properly suit our needs because of budget cuts, for example having to wait for many hours in A&E to see a doctor.

Bonus tip: If you do struggle with waiting in lines as an impulsive ADHDer, you might want to get your hands on a **sunflower lanyard**. The sunflower lanyard was created by the Hidden Disabilities team as a visible symbol for somebody to wear to communicate that they have a 'hidden' or 'invisible' disability and might require some extra support. If you wear them in certain places, such as the airport, you're able to bypass queues and use the assistance lane or sometimes even get on the plane ahead of everybody else, as a reasonable adjustment to accommodate your disability. This has been a game-changer for me as an autistic ADHDer who is a frequent traveller but who struggles with waiting, especially in noisy and sensory-overload-inducing environments.

PS: This tip was impulsively added to the book as I happened to be writing this chapter on the plane to my holiday. I hadn't previously thought to include it and it was not in my plan, but after navigating the airport this morning I decided it would be a good thing to let you know about. Told you impulsivity had its perks!!!!

In addition to this, I believe that our views around impulsivity are shaped by the misogyny that is rife within our patriarchal society. Among many other things, we have been conditioned to think that women should be caregivers, meek, mellow and polite, whereas men might be able to get away with being more boisterous, confident and loud.

Using 'risky' behaviours, such as engaging in sexual relationships, as an example, we can see the differences in how we might consider the encounter depending on whether it was a man or woman behaving in the 'impulsive' way. Of course, it is important that all of us engage in safe, protected and consensual sex; however, our opinions of men who engage in casual or 'impulsive' sex tend to be very different to those we hold of women who do the same. A man who has a one-night stand might be seen as a 'lad' or a 'legend' and praised for his behaviour, whereas a woman is seen as 'impulsive', 'improper', 'irresponsible' and might even be slut-shamed.

Similarly, a woman who decides to leave an unhappy marriage might be 'impulsive' and shamed for 'failing to protect the family unit', whereas a man might be seen as 'doing what's best for his career'.

If we look into this further, often we label a decision or behaviour as impulsive simply because we don't agree with it ourselves, or can't understand the person's reasoning – rather than it being impulsive in itself. Just because you can't see or understand the thought process that has gone into somebody else's decision does not mean that it never happened. And just because the decision or behaviour seemed sudden or impulsive to an outsider does not mean that it wasn't carefully considered beforehand. It can feel as though calling a behaviour impulsive is a way to shame somebody out of making the decision, rather than a genuine consideration of how much time they have put into weighing it up.

This shows up in the examples we shared above with misogyny, but also very frequently because of the way that we have been socialized within our capitalist society. We live and work in a world where we're told that the 'right' thing to do is do well at school, get 'good' grades, go off to study at a 'good' university, get a 'good' degree, get a 'good' corporate job, climb your way up the career ladder, and work hard every day for the rest of your life until you retire at the age of seventy (if you're lucky). Any deviance from this 'lifestyle' that we've had carefully planned out for us is seen as impulsive, no matter how carefully thought out it actually is.

Quitting your job without another one lined up? Sounds impulsive!

. . . Or maybe it is a very carefully considered decision which you believe is necessary for your mental health.

Dropping out of uni? Sounds impulsive!

... Or maybe you have discovered that university isn't the right path for you and you don't want to waste more time and money completing a degree that you don't really want.

Taking a year off work to go travelling? Sounds impulsive!

... Or maybe you have spent lots of time planning and saving up and want to experience more of what the world has to offer?

It goes without saying that all these decisions *do* need to be carefully considered; however, my point is that we see anything that deviates from 'normal' ways of living (informed by late-stage capitalism) as being more impulsive than other decisions that we might make, regardless of the time and consideration that might have gone into making the decision in question.

Imagine two people: Person A is making the decision to leave their current corporate job to start their own creative small business, and Person B is making the decision to leave their current corporate job to get a different corporate job at another company. Even if both Person A and Person B put the exact same amount of time and consideration into making the decision, in my experience it is likely that Person A would be considered more 'impulsive' than Person B. This doesn't make any sense! Equally, if Person A told two friends, Person C who is self-employed and Person D who has worked for the same company their entire life, that they are planning to leave the job to start their own business, I have found that it is more likely that Person D would label them impulsive than Person C, who has lived-experience of making that decision themselves.

All this goes to say that something being 'impulsive' is subjective and depends on the other person's frame of reference, including whether they agree with the decision you are making. We never truly know how much somebody has considered a decision, and there is no arbitrary amount of time that we 'should' take before acting or making a decision about something. Although it absolutely can be destructive and incredibly difficult to live with a brain that quickly acts on impulses, for instance when dealing with the examples listed above such as impulse spending or engaging in risky behaviours, sometimes acting quickly and impulsively is advantageous and therefore praised.

This might be in the office, making a quick business decision that allows action to be taken, or in a medical setting, trusting your instinct and making the decision to operate quickly, for example, rather than letting somebody's situation deteriorate. In those situations, we don't shame somebody for their 'impulsive' behaviour, we praise them for their ability to 'think on their feet'. (Side note that as a very literal-thinking autistic person who can struggle with sayings, I had to double and triple check that 'think on their feet' a) was the right combination of words [feet, toes . . . ?] and b) meant what I wanted it to [surely we are always thinking on our feet if we really think about it . . . well, unless we're sitting down, that is]. Anyway! Hopefully you know what I mean.) I have found that this also often depends on whether the outcome of the 'impulsive decision' is what is desired or not. If you quit your job to start your own business and it doesn't become profitable quickly, it was an 'impulsive decision', but if you start that business and turn over a million pounds in the first year then it was 'instinctive' and 'following your calling'.

How can we support ourselves with inhibition/impulse control?

As we'll explore later on in the chapter in our bigger tips, a lot of the things we (and the people around us) can do to support ourselves with inhibition/impulse control are about **adding friction** to the decision-making process. Our brains don't stop us jumping into things in the same way that other people's do, so we have to find ways of manually putting some sort of barrier into place to hold us back from going full steam ahead.

You can do this in a whole range of ways – and it's absolutely okay to expect other people to do the same thing to support you, too. After all, if, for example, a manager knows that you're prone to impulsively saying 'yes' to taking on additional work without properly considering if you have the capacity, or a friend knows that you're prone to impulsively saying 'yes' to lending them money without properly considering whether you can afford to, and they continue to ask these questions without putting some kind of barrier in for you, they are taking advantage of you. Not everybody has bad intentions – but I hope that reading this helps you to realize that asking people to tweak the ways in which they communicate with you to better support your brain is not too much to ask.

A list of things that are <u>absolutely fine</u>:

(Some of these are repeated from the previous chapter on self-monitoring because, essentially, that's what we're trying to do: build in time for us to self-monitor and work out what we think or how we feel about something, to stop us impulsively jumping in when it would be unhelpful and/or dangerous to do so.)

- Asking to have some time to consider your capacity and how much you already have on your plate before saying yes or no to a request.

- Asking to have some time to process how you feel about something somebody has said to you before responding, for example, needing some time to process how you feel after somebody has hurt you instead of rushing into accepting an apology before you've had time to work out if you're actually ready to forgive somebody.

- Asking to receive these requests or 'big' or 'important' communications via email or text message rather than verbally or face-to-face so you have that time to process and consider.

- Implementing rules to help prevent you from impulsive decision-making, such as waiting forty-eight hours before buying anything over £100 (more on finances later in the chapter!) or using a scripted phrase such as 'Thank you for asking me about XYZ. I no longer say "yes" to anything in the moment, but I will get back to you by (insert timeframe here) if it's something I'd like to do/be involved with/etc.'

- Asking to have meetings while walking instead of while sitting around a desk to prevent you from needing to 'impulsively' stand up in the middle of the discussion.

- Changing topics impulsively during a conversation because your brain is racing in lots of different directions.

- Leaning into your urges to try lots of different hobbies or hyperfixations (maybe try attending a club rather than buying all the equipment or supplies impulsively!).

- Using tools such as a 'pros and cons' table to help you consider whether something is a good idea.

- Asking for advice from trusted friends, colleagues or family members when you feel like making an impulsive decision might be a bad idea.

- Switching off your phone or deleting social media apps when you're feeling particularly impulsive (e.g. after drinking alcohol), to prevent saying/sharing anything that you might regret.

Tip 11:
Car park of ideas

By Leanne Maskell (she/her), award-winning ADHD coach and author of **ADHD An A to Z**

People with ADHD are ideas-machines, so we can sometimes get overwhelmed with wanting to do **EVERYTHING RIGHT NOW.** The 30% developmental delay in executive functioning skills means that we may experience time as 'now' or 'not now', making it hard to prioritize, delegate and plan ahead, especially when we're on the tidal wave of hyperfocus.

This is thanks to our interest-based nervous system. In contrast to neurotypical brains, which are said to be driven by importance, we are energized and motivated by **interest, novelty and adrenaline.** Our brains, especially when in hyperfocus mode, often feel like a super-whizzy racing car dragging us in circles, but with bicycle brakes, so we can't stop! Except, we can – this is where ADHD coaching comes in. By working **with** our brains instead of **against** them, we can do it all – just not all at the same time!

At ADHD Works, we train ADHD coaches to use an exercise for this called the **'car park of ideas'.**

Essentially, it's imagining your brain as a car park, with each super-important-and-must-do-right-now idea noted down and separated out into individual cars in this car park. You can draw each one out, personalizing the idea with the size and type of the car. Pink Ferraris, Lamborghinis with wings, Porsches with tents on the roof, home-made cardboard-box racing cars – go wild.

Now, we all know that it's impossible to drive more than one car at a time. Even if you were a billionaire with a garage full of racing cars, at any one time **you can only drive one**. Imagine that you start by taking the first car you want to drive, thinking ahead to plan out the journey. The rest of your ideas are waiting for you in the car park, ready to spring to life when you are – **but you are consciously driving one at a time**.

When we pick one car (or idea) to use at a time, we can then think about what we need to do and how to break it down. This involves thinking about the endpoint: how will we know when we're finished? What's at the end of the drive?

Setting this out in advance enables us to strengthen the bicycle brakes and use each idea with purpose, avoiding overwhelm. Once we're done with the first drive, we can metaphorically park it back in the car park, and perhaps pick out another to take for a spin.

This exercise helps us to counteract the dopamine-seeking parts of our brains with action: we are 'doing' something with our ideas by writing them down and holding them in one physical spot, so we don't feel under pressure to do every idea immediately or risk losing them forever.

We know they're there waiting for us, and breaking down our overwhelm like this can help us to pick the most exciting idea first, without holding ourselves to this being the only idea we will ever do!

On the following page, you can park up some of the ideas you have in your very own car park, knowing that they will be safe for you to come back to later.

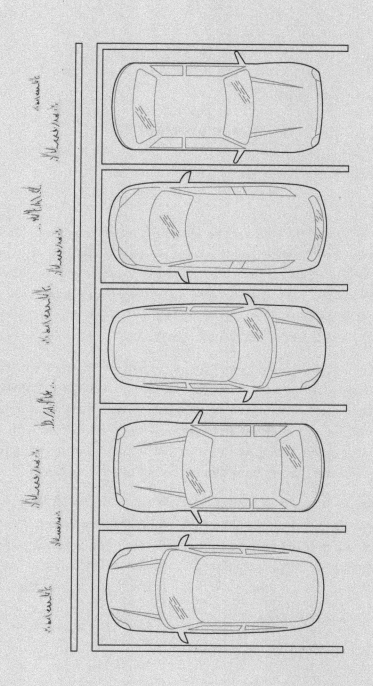

Tip 12:
Switch over, not off

My brain only has one setting:

ON.

I am always thinking about and doing a million things at a time, whirring through life (and have even previously been referred to as 'Hurricane Ellie'). While I know that resting is incredibly important (for anyone, but especially as a neurodivergent person who has a smaller battery than most people), I still find it really hard to 'switch off' or do nothing – it is just not in my nature.

In the past, whenever I would try to 'switch off' completely in the evening, at the weekend, or while on holiday, I would end up doing other impulsive things to (subconsciously) find a way to give my brain the dopamine hit that it needed. I would often come back from a holiday having booked another holiday, applied for a course, applied for a job or made other impulsive plans – not ideal!

But now I know that switching off isn't going to work for me, I can take steps to try and hold off this impulsivity by switching OVER to a different, more relaxing task, rather than trying to switch OFF completely. Some of the tasks I find helpful to switch over to are:

- **Reading a book.**

- **Learning/studying something new.**

- Doing something creative like painting or making a collage.

- Watching a film or TV series.

The trick is to find something that gives your brain just enough stimulation while still allowing you to rest from your main tasks like work or study.

Many neurodivergent folks are really bad at doing things 'just for the love of it'; we can really tie our worth to our productivity and feel like we need to be achieving something at all times, especially if we have spent a lot of our lives undiagnosed. I, for one, am seriously guilty of this – but I know the importance of giving my brain some time to rest, so **switching over** has been a game-changer for me.

Some tasks that you could switch over to when trying to rest:

- _____

- _____

- _____

- _____

- _____

Tip 13:
Do not disturb

Our next tip is incredibly simple, but often it is the smallest changes that make the biggest difference. I know I am biased, but I do think that this is one of those cases.

Let's face it: technology is a pretty big part of our lives. My screen time is incredibly high, often higher than I'd like to admit, and I'm sure many of you will feel the same. We switch between sitting in front of a medium-sized screen at work, coming home and scrolling on a smaller screen, and sometimes watching something on a bigger screen for good measure. And many of the apps on these screens are actively designed to make us want to spend even more time on them, which can sometimes take advantage of our impulsive, dopamine-seeking natures.

One way that impulsivity really creeps up for me is when I see a notification. No matter how important a task I'm completing or how focused I might be, if I see a notification pop up letting me know that a friend has commented on my picture or I have an email from an exciting brand, I immediately want to check what it is. I don't stop to think, 'Is interrupting my flow right now going to be helpful?' or 'Do I have the time to read this email at this very second?' I just see the notification pop up and click through to the app it came from before my brain has even tuned into what's going on.

The solution to this is simple – **turn the notifications off**. You can either do this manually app by app so the notifications don't come through to your phone at all (for example, turning off notifications within Instagram or Gmail), or by putting your phone on to 'Do Not Disturb' mode, which temporarily silences any notifications and shows you them once you switch it off. I personally use a combination of both: I have all notifications for social media turned off all the time, but use Do Not Disturb while I am working to stop any WhatsApp/iMessage notifications disturbing me. However, you can do whatever works best for you.

For things like work emails, for example, where it *is* important that you remember to read them at some point (without the helpful reminder from the notification), you could schedule in a slot at the start and end of every day to make sure you're still responding to them in a timely manner, without impulsively jumping to check them when you're in the middle of something important.

To get you thinking about which notifications might be unhelpful, you could keep a log of which apps you get notifications from over a twenty-four-hour period and note which ones you need to see (or are helpful to see) and which ones you don't need to see (and are unhelpful or distracting). You can then go into the settings for each app that you don't need to see notifications for and manually switch them off.

App	Number of notifications	Helpful or unhelpful?	Action (Turn off? Do not disturb?)

Tip 14:
Message monitor

As somebody who has always been very impulsive, there have been plenty of times when I have sent spur-of-the-moment text messages, which I have later (very much) regretted. (Shoutout to all the mediocre men who received multi-paragraph, heartfelt messages explaining my every thought when they let me down and/or broke my heart.) However much cringe I might feel from thinking about these messages, it turns out that this can actually be explained by science (who'd have thought it!).

Remember that dopamine 'go' signal we spoke about earlier? Well, although the research on exactly how those floods of dopamine are triggered is still very limited, one recent study found a possible link to emotional escalation. This means that events that trigger sudden and intense emotions – like panic, anger or euphoria – may trigger higher amounts of dopamine. And as we know, more dopamine = more urgency to DO SOMETHING (i.e. send a long, impulsive, heartfelt paragraph).

This research (check out the references at the back of the book if you're interested in reading more!) means that my urge to send these messages (or equally reply impulsively to comments that make me angry on social media, for example) is always going to be there – it is just the way my brain works – but equally, is a behaviour that I would very much rather move away from. Lots of people suggest using your notes app or a journal, which does go *some* way to fulfilling that need to impulsively express your every thought and feeling on whatever it is that has triggered you. However, I personally find that doing this doesn't quite scratch the itch. A lot of the 'thrill' that comes from sending these impulsive messages comes from the risk and the 'Oh my god, what have I just done?!' feeling that comes when pressing send, which just isn't there when you're typing in your notes.

One way that I've found to overcome this is having a dedicated friend (or friends) to send these impulsive messages to instead of sending them to the person I want to. I will type out the message in a fury or panic or whatever other emotion I might be feeling, exactly as I would have done if I was going to reply to somebody, but instead, send it to my designated friend. You still get the rush of typing away frantically in WhatsApp, and you still get the thrill of pressing send – just without the next day/minute/hour dread/embarrassment/cringe (thank you so much, Alyx and Charli, for volunteering to receive these and never judging my extremely over-the-top impulsive reactions).

If you're going through a tough time with work and don't want to suffer the consequences of replying angrily to your manager, or you're going through a breakup and don't want to suffer the repercussions of pouring your heart out to someone who absolutely is not worthy of your feelings, ask a friend if they'll volunteer to be your **message monitor**. (I would probably let them know beforehand so they have context for the rant that is coming their way.)

Tip 15:
Managing your finances

By Tanisha Cro, autistic and ADHD finance manager and financial coach

Whether you believe money is good or evil, it is a necessary tool for creating the life we want to live. Money can give us freedom, experiences, safety, and the power to say no to things that don't serve us – so it's essential that we look after it.

As a financial coach who works with many neurodivergent clients, some of the most common money struggles they report are with impulsive spending (especially takeaways and special interest-related purchases) and trouble with planning ahead for future purchases, i.e. annual subscriptions.

There are a couple of things that you can do to support yourself with inhibition/impulse control when it comes to money:

Get the system to work for you!
Rather than trying to fight the system, sometimes it is better to just find a better system. Is the bank that you're using helping you keep on top of everything, or could they be doing better? Some features that can be helpful for busy brains are:

- Instant notifications for whenever money enters or leaves your current account.

- Real-time balance updates.

- Upcoming payment reminders.

- Places to set money aside automatically, which can be locked (use out of sight, out of mind to grow your savings).

- Web Chat features — avoiding those awful phone calls!

- Add dopamine trackers, colours, fancy pens and stickers, checklists and small goals, visual spending breakdown or a rewards system.

- Gamify your money — add challenge, competitions and rewards to spice things up.

Check whether there are any tools you're not making the most of, look for a new bank or let your current bank know they could be doing better. The more of us that speak up, the more that will change. Some of the new challenger banks, such as Monzo and Starling, implement these features, and so might be helpful to check out.

Add friction to purchases!
It is easier than ever to make big impulsive purchases. The idea is to add friction to try and override the impulse. Try:

Short-term

- Delete all saved bank details from online shopping sites or auto-fill passwords.

- Write notes on your debit cards such as 'Do I really need this?' or 'Saving for XYZ!'

- Stick Post-its on the wall near where you spend time on your phone or computer or have a visual reminder of what meaningful thing you're saving your money for.

- Before you purchase anything, make a habit of brain-dumping in a journal – why do you want to buy this, and will it add to your life? What are you saying no to by purchasing this?

- Mute/unfollow creators or brands that tempt you, especially if you are vulnerable to sales and marketing tactics.

- Set up different accounts for where your money goes in and spending comes out.

- Leave online shopping for twenty-four hours in the cart before buying – you sometimes get rewards and discounts for doing this!

- Have funds allocated specifically for fun/splurge money, which you can spend completely guilt-free on whatever you want.

Long-term

- Identify your emotional state when you have the urge to spend – are you bored? Under-stimulated?

Over-stimulated? What is your brain saying to you? Are you stressed?

- Be honest about what your brain is actually craving — can you get your dopamine hit from somewhere else, like exercise? Are you craving connection or comfort?

- Find an alternative coping mechanism — what could give you that same feeling but is easier on your money? Go for a walk/call a friend/play with a pet?

Just start with one small step and allow yourself to let go of the expectation that there is one perfect tool/app out there and you will probably go through many different tools to keep the novelty and interest alive. That is okay! Finally, I'd like to finish by saying again and again — it was never a waste of money if it was important to you, so don't let anyone tell you otherwise!

Inhibition/impulse control recap

Our third executive functioning skill, **inhibition/impulse control**, is defined as the ability to resist impulsive urges and hold back from inappropriate or disruptive behaviours. It describes our brain's ability to stop and think about whether something is a good idea, rather than jumping straight in, and involves being able to control one's attention, behaviour, thoughts and/or emotions to override a strong internal predisposition or external lure, and instead do what's more appropriate or needed. Sometimes, this is a handy skill to stop us rushing into risky or unhelpful situations; however, as we've explored throughout the chapter, there are other times when thinking and acting quickly can work to our advantage.

In this chapter, we have explored:

- What inhibition/impulse control is.

- The systems which have affected the way we think about inhibition/impulse control.

- Some ways we can support ourselves with inhibition/impulse control.

- 5 things to consider putting in place for your inhibition/impulse control.

Your takeaway box

- Impulsivity is subjective. Nobody else knows how much thought or consideration has gone into a decision you make, and their calling you 'impulsive' might be more of a reflection of their disagreement with your decision rather than the thoroughness of your consideration.

- Sometimes, being prone to acting on our impulses can be a good thing. It allows us to act quickly, pivot, and stay ahead of others who might spend longer deliberating whether something is a good idea or not. When it is safe to do so and doesn't have financial or safety risks, it can actually be beneficial for us to lean into our impulsive nature.

- Adding friction to decision-making processes can help us to hold back from making impulsive decisions. Our brains don't stop us jumping into things in the same way that other people's do, so we have to find ways of manually putting some sort of barrier in place to hold us back from going full steam ahead. You can do this in a whole range of ways, and it's absolutely okay to expect other people to do the same thing to support you, too.

4

Emotional regulation

Just before I discovered that I was an autistic ADHDer, when I knew my previous diagnoses of generalized anxiety disorder, panic disorder and agoraphobia didn't accurately describe my experience and was, therefore, looking for other explanations, I went through a phase of being convinced that I had either bipolar disorder or borderline personality disorder (BPD). This was because so many of my struggles came from the **intensity** and **up-and-down nature** of my emotions. I have always felt as though I'm either **really** happy or **really** sad, with not much in between, and bipolar and BPD were the only explanations for this rollercoaster of quickly changing, intense emotions that I'd ever heard spoken about.

Since my lightbulb moment, I've discovered that these diagnoses don't actually fit my experience and that the differences I have in my emotional regulation abilities are actually down to being an autistic ADHDer. ADHD means that I struggle to regulate my emotions in the same way that other people can, and being an undiagnosed (and, therefore, unsupported) autistic person in a world that was never designed for me meant that I was frequently driving myself into states of burnout, during which I'd feel my emotions even more intensely.

Since sharing my story online, I've heard about so many people going through the same journey of thinking their challenges with emotional regulation were down to a mental health condition or different type of neurodivergence before discovering their autism and ADHD, and maybe it's even something you can relate to, too.

In this chapter, we will explore:

- What is emotional regulation?

- Which systems have affected the way we think about emotional regulation?

- How can we support ourselves with emotional regulation?

- 5 things to consider putting in place for your emotional regulation.

We, as a society, are not used to seeing public or outward displays of emotion – and this is something that needs to change.

Although some emotions might be uncomfortable to experience, they are all completely valid and a normal part of being a human being.

What is emotional regulation?

Emotional regulation is defined as the ability to recognize, understand and effectively manage your emotions and reactions to different situations. *Psychology Today* describes it as 'the ability to exert control over one's own emotional state, [which] may involve behaviours such as rethinking a challenging situation to reduce anger or anxiety, hiding visible signs of sadness or fear, or focusing on reasons to feel happy or calm'. As someone who experiences these differences in emotional regulation, I have always felt my feelings **really** deeply and struggled to keep them under control. For you this might show up in ways like:

- Being prone to losing your temper.

- Experiencing rapid mood swings.

- Having trouble steering your moods, and so feeling stuck or unable to make yourself feel better when experiencing negative emotions.

- Spiralling into intense sadness when one small thing goes wrong.

- Feeling really overwhelmed by your emotions.

- Having very intense periods of sobbing when feeling unhappy.

- Having a hard time focusing on anything else but emotions or an emotional situation.

- Finding it difficult to calm yourself down, even if you know the situation isn't that significant.

- Having reactions that other people might deem 'out of proportion' to what has happened/been said.

In an article for *ADDitude*, Dr Russell Barkley explains that emotional dysregulation (I personally don't love the use of the word dysregulation because it suggests that we have a deficit or disorder, when, under the neurodiversity paradigm, we would instead say that we just have **differences** in our emotional regulation) has been shown to uniquely predict the following:

- Social rejection in children with ADHD.

- Interpersonal hostility and marital dissatisfaction in adults with ADHD.

- Greater parenting stress and family conflict in parents of children with ADHD.

- Greater stress in parents with ADHD.

- Road rage, incidences of driving under the influence (DUIs), and crash risks during driving.

- Job dismissals and workplace interpersonal problems.

- Dating/cohabiting relationship conflict.

- Impulse buying.

- Poor finances.

Although a lot of the examples above make emotional regulation differences seem like a complete curse (which they often can be), I've personally always said that my ability to feel things so deeply is both my biggest blessing **and** my biggest curse. Yes, the 'bad' or negative feelings feel *really* bad – but that means that I feel the 'good' or positive feelings really intensely, too. This can show up in ways like:

- Feeling really intense joy when listening to my favourite music.

- Being overwhelmed with pride and happiness when my loved ones achieve something.

- Loving and caring for my friends and family so deeply.

- Getting really excited about things that other people might deem 'small'.

- Feeling really happy when engaging with my special interests.

Sometimes, differences in emotional regulation (for example, for autistic people) can even show up in us appearing to have no emotional reactions in situations where they would be expected. This might include:

- Not crying when something sad happens because we might take longer to process things.

- Not smiling when we feel happy because we don't show our emotions in the same ways as neurotypical people.

- Not responding to other people's emotions in the same way that other people would because we might struggle to understand and recognize non-verbal cues or facial expressions.

- Not being able to identify how we feel about something because of alexithymia (which is defined as the inability to recognize or describe one's own emotions).

Barkley puts some of the emotional regulation difficulties that ADHDers have down to what he calls **emotional impulsiveness** (EI) and believes that it is, therefore, linked to the hyperactive/impulsive nature of ADHDers. Emotional regulation challenges are not currently part of the diagnostic criteria for ADHD, but it is becoming more and more widely recognized that this is a major part of the experiences of ADHDers and otherwise neurodivergent folks.

Research has shown that emotion regulation differences are prevalent in ADHD throughout the lifespan (i.e. ADHDers of all ages) and are a 'major contributor to impairment'. (Again, not a huge fan of 'impairment'; maybe we could reframe this as 'major disabling factor'.) The same study suggested that these emotional regulation differences might arise from our difficulty in orienting towards, recognizing or allocating our attention to emotional stimuli.

As well as ADHDers experiencing differences in the way we are able to regulate our emotions, it can be a very common experience for a whole range of neurodivergent people. This includes those with bipolar disorder and borderline personality disorder, as mentioned above, as well as autistic people, dyslexic people and people with depression. Remember that if the way that you think, learn, behave, communicate, process information or feel emotions diverges from societal norms, you are neurodivergent – and, therefore, anyone who experiences emotions differently falls under the neurodivergent umbrella.

Which systems have affected the way we think about emotional regulation?

I think a big part of what we fail to remember about emotional regulation is that emotions are a natural part of being human – even the big, messy, 'difficult' or 'unpleasant' ones. In the Western world – especially in British culture – we have been taught to 'keep a stiff upper lip' and control our emotions to an almost impossible degree. Especially when it comes to negative emotions, the general consensus seems to be 'Don't show any emotion in any circumstance, no matter how much you're struggling or what you're going through.' On the one hand, we're encouraged to open up about our mental health and talk to people, but on the other hand we're frowned upon if we ever answer the question 'How are you?' with anything less than 'good, thanks' or even 'fine'. This, however, isn't objectively how we 'should' be able to regulate our emotions, and certainly isn't the case in all cultures. As **Yasmin Johal** (she/her), autistic content creator, explains:

South Asians live in and thrive in community, so it's very normal for us to process our feelings with and around our loved ones and not shy away from our emotions. In particular, displays of grief in South Asian communities can be very overwhelming. Of course, grief is a very intense emotion in any culture – but it's the norm for grieving South Asians to wail loudly and extensively, at home, at the temple, and at the funeral; to release their emotions in the most cathartic but heartbreaking way. There are no awkward glances from others in attendance, just the utmost empathy and understanding of what has been lost. The sniffles I've heard at English funerals, in comparison, are quite jarring to me, but I understand it's just different cultures responding in the only way they know or have been taught.

This also links to some further characteristics of White supremacy culture, as defined by Tema Okun (you can find more on these characteristics in **What defines our views of executive functioning?, page 19**): The first of these is **objectivity**, which assigns value to 'rational' or 'logical' thinking, while invalidating and shaming anything considered 'emotional'. This means that anybody who shows or expresses emotions or is thought to 'lead with their heart' is seen as wrong or lesser – even when faced with a situation that is **bound** to cause or trigger a lot of emotion. Objectivity undermines the fact that emotional intelligence is a very real and valuable skill and that, as human beings, we are naturally complex and emotional beings.

How objectivity affects the way we see emotional regulation and executive functioning:

- Objectivity means that we see those who outwardly express emotions as irrational or illogical, and, therefore, defines what we consider to be emotional regulation vs 'dysregulation'.

- We often do not consider the circumstances or situations that might be causing someone to be emotionally 'dysregulated', even when the emotion shown is a perfectly valid response to those circumstances.

- In the diagnostic criteria for ADHD and autism, we don't allow for subjective experiences or reasons *why* people might be struggling. For example, if someone is going through an especially hard time, they might find task initiation, planning or organization particularly difficult, or have a whole load of emotions that feel too big to regulate, but this reasoning behind differences or changes isn't considered.

Second, **fear of (open) conflict** also impacts the way we think about emotional regulation. In order to further protect each person's individual comfort in cultures where White supremacy is prevalent, we often experience a fear of open conflict. Disagreements are often not voiced – and those who do voice concerns are often silenced in order to 'keep the peace'. This means that if somebody does raise an issue that causes discomfort, the most likely response is to blame the person for raising the issue, rather than to look at the issue which is actually causing the problem. This can result in labelling emotions as irrational, calling people 'difficult' if they speak openly about issues that are caused, insisting that people prioritize being 'polite' over being honest, and having strict, unspoken rules about what should and should not be spoken about (all of which is especially difficult to navigate as an autistic person).

How fear of (open) conflict affects the way we see emotional regulation and executive functioning:

- Neurodivergent people might feel as though they cannot raise concerns or questions about the way things are done, or express their emotions visibly, for fear of it being seen to be 'causing conflict'.

- When people do ask to be accommodated for their executive functioning differences, they might be labelled 'difficult' for 'disturbing the status quo'.

- Tone policing often comes into play here, where politeness is valued over the importance of the topic somebody feels strongly about. This might lead to somebody being considered to be 'emotionally dysregulated' rather than taking on board their concerns.

In my opinion, the way we perceive emotional regulation is also very closely tied to misogyny and our patriarchal society. Women and people marginalized for their gender are often called 'irrational' or 'emotional' if they outwardly express their emotions – while simultaneously being socialized under patriarchy to be 'soft' and 'gentle'. We are considered to be less 'reliable' or 'professional' because we are more likely to outwardly express our emotions than cis men might be.

However, it is not just women and people marginalized for their gender who 'lose' in a patriarchal society – we all do. Under patriarchy, men are typically expected to display only 'harder' emotions such as anger, and to suppress any 'softer' or empathetic emotions. These societal expectations can shape **all** our perceptions of which emotions are 'acceptable' or 'appropriate' for us to feel and express, and we're led to believe that an outward display of more vulnerable emotions, like sadness, fear or anxiety, is 'weak' – with men who express these emotions even being considered 'feminine'. The result of all this is that women are considered to be weak or overly emotional, and men are left without the tools or language to be able to feel, process, describe and express their emotions in a healthy way.

How can we support ourselves with emotional regulation?

I think there are two big things to remember here. The first is that there is no such thing as a 'bad' or 'wrong' feeling. Although some emotions might be uncomfortable to experience, they are all completely valid and a normal part of being a human being. Sadness is a perfectly valid response to an upsetting experience, anger (when expressed in a safe way) is a good reminder of when something doesn't align with us, and anxiety is our body's way of letting us know that something is important to us. There are no emotions that we should aim to completely eradicate or just 'never feel', because all emotions serve a purpose. We don't need to shame ourselves for having a human reaction to our circumstances.

This is particularly true when we live in a world where there is often a lot to feel upset, angry or anxious about. We are living through a cost-of-living crisis, watching wars unfold before our eyes, while witnessing the effects that the climate crisis is having on our planet. We see injustice all around us, and we are exposed to it in a way that humans have never been before, thanks to our almost constant use of social media, smartphones and the internet. It is to be expected that we might be feeling some kind of way about all of that – and it's important that we do.

The second thing that I think it's important we remember is that it's okay to show our emotions. We don't have to hide everything away and spend our whole lives pretending that everything is fine and we're completely unbothered and unfazed by everything that is happening around us. Opening up and outwardly expressing our emotions can feel scary and vulnerable, but in the words of Brené Brown, 'Staying vulnerable is a risk we have to take if we want to experience connection.'

Personally, I am a big crier. I think it's partially down to my struggles with emotional regulation, partially down to my communication differences as an autistic person, and partially down to the fact that I am living in a world that is almost always overwhelming for my neurodivergent brain. Whatever the reason, the point is that I cry **a**

lot. Many of the times that I'm crying, I don't actually need sympathy or support or anything at all from the people around me. For me, it's not a sign that I'm distraught, or breaking down, or having a really awful time; it's simply my body's way of communicating that 'there is a lot going on right now'. But because we've all been socialized to hide our emotions whenever possible, we've somehow learned that if somebody *is* crying, it must be something **really** bad for it to have gotten to the point that they aren't able to suppress their tears. This means that when I cry (most days), often the people around me at the time don't know how to respond. They assume that something really awful has happened, so they might stop and stare, ask me if I'm okay, or make a big fuss. In reality, I don't want this fuss; I just want to be able to communicate in my own way, even if there are tears involved.

We, as a society, are not used to seeing public or outward displays of emotion – and this is something that needs to change. Below are a few ways that we can start to make that shift happen, whether that's as the 'criers' ourselves or the people around us who know it's okay not to bat an eyelid at somebody openly expressing their emotions.

A list of things that are <u>absolutely fine</u>:

- Crying in public.

- Flapping your hands when you experience a lot of joy.

- Asking to have some time out to process your emotions when they become overwhelming.

- Admitting that you're having a hard time instead of pretending that everything is A-okay.

- Needing to use tools such as the Emotion Sensation Feeling Wheel (more on this on page 113) to work out which physical feelings in your body relate to which emotions.

- Having a hard time regulating your tone of voice when your emotions are high.

- Asking people, 'How are you?' and then when they reply with the usual 'good' or 'fine', asking again, 'But *really*, how are you?'

- Feeling and expressing anger in safe and non-hurtful ways, like screaming into your pillow or ranting to a friend.

- Not being able to immediately 'get over' something or somebody that has upset you and needing to take some time to process it.

- Actually feeling your feelings, rather than thinking that you have to suppress them.

Tip 16:
5, 4, 3, 2, 1

A big factor in feeling our emotions are impossible to regulate is that we frequently get stuck in our heads. Especially when you have a busy, hyperactive brain, it's incredibly easy to get stuck in a spiral of ruminating thoughts, going over and over the situation, what you did say, what you could have said, what you could have done differently, what the other person might be thinking, how you might have been misunderstood, what the outcome is going to be, and so on, and so on. The impulsive and hyperactive nature of my brain, combined with the trauma I have from growing up as an undiagnosed and unsupported autistic person, means that I frequently get caught up in these rumination cycles.

To pull ourselves out of this spiral, we can use a **mindfulness technique** to force our awareness **out** of our busy brains and **into** our bodies. I know, I know. Mindfulness feels very wishy-washy when you're a black-and-white, literal processor and feels completely unattainable when you're a busy-brained ADHDer whose thoughts are constantly racing around at a million miles per hour. But trust me when I say that this very simple, very logical technique is a **game-changer**.

When you notice that you're stuck in a busy-brain rumination spiral, you're going to do a really simple grounding exercise called 5, 4, 3, 2, 1. This means identifying and listing:

- **5 things you can see.**

- **4 things you can touch.**

- **3 things you can hear.**

- **2 things you can smell.**

- **1 thing you can taste.**

Doing this helps shift your focus **away** from any anxiety-provoking thoughts and **into** the present moment. As Calm, the mindfulness and meditation app, explain on their website: 'The 5, 4, 3, 2, 1 method works because it engages multiple senses, requiring you to concentrate on the **present environment** rather than dwell on anxiety-inducing thoughts. This interrupts the fight or flight response, calming the nervous system and reducing symptoms of anxiety or stress almost immediately.'

By focusing on your senses and the things happening in the present moment, you're letting your brain know that there is no immediate threat and it therefore doesn't need to be operating in fight or flight mode. After all, if there **was** an immediate danger (like, for example, a lion chasing after you), you wouldn't have the chance to stop and think, 'Hmmm, what can I taste right now?' and so, in doing so, you're allowing your brain to recognize that it's okay to down-regulate the stress response. This pulls you away from the rumination cycles, and therefore makes your emotions feel a whole lot less overwhelming.

Here is a template for filling in your 5, 4, 3, 2, 1. Feel free to take a photo of this and use it as your phone screen wallpaper as a frequent reminder to bring yourself back to the present moment.

- **What are 5 things I can see?**

  1. _____

  2. _____

  3. _____

  4. _____

  5. _____

- **What are 4 things I can touch?**

  1. _____

  2. _____

  3. _____

  4. _____

- **What are 3 things I can hear?**

  1. _____

  2. _____

  3. _____

- What are 2 things I can smell?

1. _____

2. _____

- What is 1 thing I can taste?

1. _____

Tip 17:
Reframing rejection

It has been reported that nearly one in three ADHDers say that the hardest part of living with ADHD is something called **Rejection Sensitive Dysphoria**, or RSD. Rejection Sensitive Dysphoria, first coined by Dr William Dodson in 2017, explains the way in which ADHDers are triggered to feel **extreme pain** when experiencing any real or perceived rejection. This might show up in response to being teased, receiving negative feedback, feeling like somebody is upset with you, or that you're not good enough in some way.

Research has suggested this extreme emotional pain is a result of the differences in brain functioning of ADHDers. It has been suggested that the 'negative effects associated with rejection or even perceived rejection are not easily processed by the brain, resulting in an intense nervous system response'.

One example that I gave in *unmasked* of how RSD shows up for me is that I will often jump to the conclusion that I am being rejected – even when, in reality, that most likely is not the case. As an example, if two friends were having a conversation just out of earshot, but I just about heard my name being mentioned, my brain would automatically think that they must be saying something bad about me, that they didn't like me, or that I had done something wrong. In reality, it's just as likely (if not more likely!) that they'd be saying something positive about me, but my brain always reverts to assuming rejection without taking this into account.

Any negative feedback (or even neutral feedback that is perceived by our brain as negative!) feels like a personal attack, a complete rejection, and can completely throw our emotions off balance. This means that an important part of learning to regulate our emotions as ADHDers (and otherwise neurodivergent folks – I think **everybody** is prone to thinking the worst and perceiving feedback as negative) is finding a way to jump in and stop our brain from racing to the worst conclusions. Or, even if they **do** jump to those conclusions, finding ways to question them and pull ourselves out of it.

One way that we can do this is by doing some self-coaching. I first learned about the framework below when training to be an ADHD coach with ADHD Works, and have found it incredibly useful in getting to the 'truth' of a situation rather than the worst-case scenario that my brain often jumps to. The questions that we want to work through are:

1. **What is the thought that is bothering me?**
   Here you want to be **completely** honest and brain-dump all the absolute worst thoughts that are racing around your brain. It might feel embarrassing or uncomfortable to admit the extremities of your thoughts but the more honest you can get, the more you're going to be able to actually work on reframing it. Nobody is going to read it – it's just for you!

   For example, if you've had a slight disagreement with your partner you might say: '*I feel like I'm the worst person in the entire world, and no one will ever love me.*'

```
┌─────────────────────────────────┐
│                                 │
│                                 │
│                                 │
│                                 │
│                                 │
└─────────────────────────────────┘
```

2. What proof do I have for this thought?

Here you're going to list all the things that have
triggered your brain into feeling that way.

That might be: 'My partner is upset with me because I
forgot about our anniversary.'

```
┌─────────────────────────────────┐
│                                 │
│                                 │
│                                 │
│                                 │
│                                 │
└─────────────────────────────────┘
```

3. What would be the result of me choosing to believe this thought?

Next, you're going to list out all the things
that happen as a result of you choosing to believe
the thought that your brain is providing you with.

This could be: 'I will feel bad. I will pull away from my
partner. I will cut myself off from other people. I will
beat myself up about it. I will start to doubt all my other
relationships', etc.'

```
┌─────────────────────────────────┐
│                                 │
│                                 │
│                                 │
│                                 │
│                                 │
└─────────────────────────────────┘
```

4. What is the absolute worst-case scenario if this thought is true? How would I deal with that?

Here you're going to indulge all your brain's chaos and write out what would happen in the absolute worst-case scenario. Hopefully, in doing so, you will see that even if it does come to that (which is incredibly unlikely), you will survive. This takes the power away from the big scary thought because we can see that it wouldn't be the complete end of the world.

For example, your worst-case scenario might be: 'My partner breaks up with me and I will deal with that by giving them some space, going to see my friends, going to stay with my parents for a few days, running myself a long, candle-lit bath, or screaming my heart out to break-up songs.' (No judgement here.)

5. What is an opposite thought that I could choose to believe instead?

After indulging those anxious fantasies, we're going to write down the complete opposite thought of our original one, which, by this point, might seem a bit more rational.

If our original thought was: '*I feel like I'm the worst person in the entire world, and no one will ever love me,*' **the opposite would be:** '*I am a good person, and I am loved.*'.

6. What proof do I have for my opposite thought?

Finally, we're going to list all (yes, **all**) the proof we have for this new thought. In doing so, we can look at the situation more rationally and see that, okay, we might have made a mistake, and, okay, our partner might be a little bit upset with us for a while. But, in the whole grand scheme of things, everything is going to be okay. We're not a terrible person, we aren't going to die alone, and the world isn't going to end. To quote one of my absolute favourite sayings (which I actually have tattooed across my back), 'It's just a bad day, not a bad life.'

Tip 18:
Sampling sobriety

By Lewis Middleton, ADHD and autistic social media manager (and my little brother! Very proud sister moment)

I've been sober for one year and counting. The impact that sobriety has had on my emotional regulation and general well-being, as someone recently diagnosed with ADHD and in the process of realizing I'm *quite possibly* autistic too, has been almost beyond belief. Who would have thought that regularly consuming depressant chemicals would make you feel bad?!

I always thought that my relationship with alcohol was healthy and never questioned the role it played in my mental health or my ability to regulate my emotions. 'I could easily stop if I wanted to' or 'I've had a stressful week – it just helps to take the edge off' was the message I'd often try and convince myself. However, the reality was that, from the ages of eighteen to twenty-two, my life revolved around drinking. My weeks used to follow a pretty similar pattern: Monday to Wednesday, I'd be hungover and feeling low. Then as soon as Thursday evening came around, I'd be straight back to having pints until Sunday evening. I couldn't just have the one or two pints, though. I had to pour as many as possible down my neck and get blackout drunk **every single time**.

In December 2022, I started to realize that my alcohol consumption was becoming a problem. It was affecting my relationships with family, who'd spend their weekends worrying if I was okay and what time I was going to stumble through the door. In myself, as much as I tried to deny it, I knew the way I was living just wasn't right. I decided that I needed to make a change.

I had my last blowout on New Year's Eve 2022. I had my last ever alcoholic drink on 1 January 2023, at 2.30 a.m. in Popworld. And from that point, I haven't looked back.

Getting through the first couple of weeks was really tough. I'd be sat at home on Friday and Saturday nights wondering what to do with myself, and the 0% beers just weren't hitting the same – but I stayed resilient and kept searching for videos with #Sobriety on TikTok to try and reaffirm all the mental and physical benefits people had spoken about.

A few people have asked me what helped me stop drinking for good in those first few weeks, so here are some of my best, most practical tips:

- Give yourself a good excuse not to drink if you're in a social setting. Say you've got to drive home. Say you've got to pick your sibling up from the airport. People will stop nagging you!

- Make sure you do something with your mornings when you'd normally be hungover in bed. It'll make you realize what you're missing.

- 0% alternatives serve a purpose for the first few weeks. You'll find that over time, the craving for alcohol will just disappear.

Now that I'm sober, I don't have to spend the first half of my week fighting my hangovers – and the subsequent low mood and extreme emotional dysregulation that came with them. I don't have to deal with the debilitating anxiety of opening my banking apps on a Sunday morning to see how many drinks I've bought for complete strangers. And now, I can actually do things I want to do with my weekend without being hungover. It's amazing.

More importantly, I've noticed that my general self-confidence has increased tenfold, as someone who previously struggled with managing my anxiety. I used to think that I needed to have two or three pints to loosen up and socialize. I've realized that alcohol was just a tool to help me mask. I feel like I can be myself now. I might not be the loudest person in the pub any more, but that wasn't me in the first place.

At the time of writing, I'm fifty-four weeks sober – and I can honestly say that I've never felt better, or more emotionally regulated, in my life. I'll never touch a drop of alcohol again. The temptation isn't there any more.

Sobriety isn't for everyone. Ideally, I'd be able to drink responsibly and call it a night. But that's just not going to happen for me as an ADHDer with impulsive tendencies. If you're somebody who shares similar experiences to mine, or struggles with emotional regulation that is heightened by drinking alcohol, maybe it's time to take a look at your relationship with alcohol and really ask yourself if it's doing you any good.

Tip 19:
Automatic writing

I've never been one for 'journalling' because, similarly to mindfulness, it all just felt a bit wishy-washy. As someone who is a chronic perfectionist, I felt like I was carefully monitoring what I was putting on the page, trying to ensure that if some (imaginary) reader got their hands on it, they would know how 'mature' and 'regulated' and 'reasonable' I was, rather than actually just brain-dumping all my raw, uncomfortable, **REAL** feelings. However, that all changed when I was introduced to **automatic writing** by KR Moorhead (they/them), a neurodivergent and genderqueer writer and educator, while studying one of their creative writing courses. KR shared with us an amended version of both the 'Morning Pages' technique outlined by Julia Cameron in her infamous book *The Artist's Way* and a technique shared by Andrew Cowan in *The Art of Writing Fiction*.

As Cowan explains, 'The practice of "automatic writing" . . . is a technique by which you might reveal to yourself what is going on in the back of your mind, the stuff you aren't consciously aware of, the stuff of your unconscious – the stuff, in a sense, that you don't know you know.' The idea here is that we're not thinking about how we 'should' be feeling or what we 'should' be thinking, but instead we're letting our actual emotions (however messy, raw, uncomfortable, suppressed or overwhelming they might be) pour out on to the page.

When practising automatic writing, you're going to set a timer for how long you're going to write. I recommend starting with ten minutes, but if that feels too daunting for you, you could start with five minutes, or even two (it's likely that once you get started, more and more stuff will pour out of you, but we don't need to scare ourselves off by setting too big a target). Once you have set your timer, you're going to begin writing and not stop for the entire length of time. It might be helpful to start with a prompt like 'I want to talk about . . .' or, 'I wish somebody understood that . . .' but once you've set off, it doesn't matter what you write, which tangents you head off on, or whether it makes any sense whatsoever; all that matters is that you **just keep writing**.

If you run out of things to write about (unlikely with a busy ADHD brain!), then you can just write, 'I don't have anything else to write about', or 'I have nothing more to say', or even, 'this is a silly exercise' over and over again until something else pops into your brain.

The rules that Andrew Cowan outlines in *The Art of Writing Fiction* are paraphrased below:

- **It's okay if your writing is illegible or doesn't have proper grammar and punctuation.**

- **It's okay if your writing feels clumsy or clichéd.**

- **It's okay to repeat yourself or even contradict yourself.**

- **It's okay to write nonsense or 'rubbish'.**

- **It's okay to write anything that you want.**

- It's okay if you go completely off the point.

- But you must write without a moment's pause for the entire amount of time.

Set yourself a task of carving out some time to do this automatic writing every day, or even grabbing a notepad and writing at any time as an emergency response when you can feel your emotions becoming dysregulated or overwhelming.

Tip 20:
Why did this upset me?

By Josephine Knechtli (she/her), AuDHD clinical hypnotherapist and rapid transformational coach

When triggers first appear, they can be a source of overwhelm and discomfort — but we can utilize them as a means of connecting and understanding ourselves. I always seek to approach triggers as a mirror:

What am I responding to, and what can I learn about myself from this experience?

Through this understanding, it's like I am turning on a light in a dark room to gain full clarity on what's happening and how I can best support myself.

Sometimes, we can feel fear when triggered. Fear stems from not having all the information we need. By getting curious, we can access the answers and understanding that places us in a position of power. Understanding gives us the tools to make choices to respond to triggers in a way that feels supportive instead of scary.

A trigger is an emotional response to something outside of us. We are often emotionally responding in ways that are tied to past experiences. Knowing this gives us an invitation to process and rewire our responses to be relevant to who we are today. The mind is here to move us from pain towards pleasure, and so pushes us into action when we experience a trigger. This is key, as it shows that our mind and body are not against us, they are here to keep us alive.

What's fascinating is that emotions are energy in motion. We do not **think** emotions; we **feel** them within our body. This is why it is important to meet triggers with a physical movement to diffuse the intensity of that energy. Movement allows the energy to be released, clearing space for us to understand and process what has happened.

When you notice that you are triggered, take a shake break. Whether it's your hands or hips – allow that movement to take place. Notice the shift you feel immediately; how great does it feel to make a choice to support yourself here?

Next, we want to take a double breath in – further telling your body that you are here, and you are safe. Then, take the time to ask yourself the following four questions:

1. **What is actually happening here?**
   Identify the reality of the situation and break down what is really going on.

2. **What am I feeling as a result?**
   What physical and emotional sensations are showing up for you?

3. **What am I actually reacting to?**
   Which specific part of what has happened is triggering you? Is it something you don't like about yourself, something that resonates with your past, or something you feel very strongly about?

4. What meaning am I placing upon the trigger?

Is this relevant to who I am today or an invitation to unravel and resolve this historical response? We have the right to choose, always. By deciding to identify and work through the things that trigger us, we are turning what used to be a trigger into a point of being able to understand and show up for ourselves differently.

For example, we don't get invited to an event we would love to be involved with.

- Notice the reaction that takes place – what emotion are you feeling?

- Where is that emotion within your body – what is the message here?

- How can you choose to respond to this emotion in a way that supports you, away from judgement for yourself?

Your triggers are parts of yourself that are asking for attention. A curious approach to triggers allows us to understand ourselves and reclaim our power.

Remind yourself, 'Triggers are not happening to me; they are happening with me – I hold the right to decide.'

Emotional regulation recap

Our fourth executive functioning skill, **emotional regulation**, is defined as the ability to recognize, understand and effectively manage our emotions and reactions to different situations. It describes our ability (or not) to exert control over our own emotional state, which might include things like rethinking a challenging situation to reduce anxiety, being able to take a deep breath to regulate our anger, hiding visible signs of sadness or fear from the people around us, or being able to pull ourselves out of tricky emotions. There are times when it is helpful for us to regulate our emotions so that we feel in control of the way we are feeling and can stop ourselves from getting stuck in bouts of low mood or anxious spirals. However, as a society, I believe that we need to be more accepting of visible displays of emotion. It's okay to feel big feelings, and it's okay to show those feelings to the people around us – whether they are more positive or negative emotions.

In this chapter, we have explored:

- What emotional regulation is.

- The systems which have affected the way we think about emotional regulation.

- Some ways we can support ourselves with emotional regulation.

- 5 things to consider putting in place for your emotional regulation.

Your takeaway box

- There is no such thing as a 'bad' or 'wrong' emotion. Some feelings are more positive, and some feelings are more negative, but they all serve a purpose. Yes, there are some emotions which might feel uncomfortable to experience, but they are all completely valid and a normal part of being a human being. There are no emotions which we should feel the need to eradicate, or shame ourselves for feeling.

- It's okay to express your emotions outwardly – even if they are not particularly positive ones. You don't have to put on a brave face or downplay your feelings, and you don't have to intellectualize your emotions to the point that you don't even get the chance to feel them at all. Sometimes, allowing yourself to fully submit to a feeling is the most cathartic and effective way to process it.

- Most of the techniques that we can use to help regulate our emotions involve finding a way to pull ourselves out of the automatic spiralling and catastrophizing of emotions that our brains are prone to. This might look like taking a deep breath, pulling ourselves back into the moment or asking ourselves questions to help rationalize our thoughts and feelings. It's important to remember that even if your emotions are dysregulated or overwhelming, they are still valid. Our aim isn't to shame ourselves for feeling that way to begin with; it's to find ways of making them feel more manageable.

5

Flexibility

One of my very favourite stories that my parents often tell me about my childhood is perhaps a great way to introduce this chapter on flexibility. By the time I was around four years old, my parents had quickly learned that they couldn't say the word McDonald's out loud. This was because if they had mentioned in passing that 'if you're a good girl today, we might be able to stop for a McDonald's on the way home', then I would take it as gospel and never let them hear the end of it. This is just one example of how my differences or struggles with flexibility have shown up throughout my life as someone who takes things very literally, sees things in quite a black-and-white way, doesn't cope well with change and likes to have things planned out in advance.

Being 'flexible' is something that is incredibly important in an ever-changing world, to allow us to keep up with changing demands, changing expectations, changing plans, and the people around us who are constantly changing, too. However, for some of the reasons mentioned above and a whole load more we'll explore throughout the chapter, it's something that can be very tricky for neurodivergent folks who rely on structure, sameness and routine.

In this chapter, we will explore:

- What is flexibility?

- Which systems have affected the way we think about flexibility?

- How can we support ourselves with flexibility?

- 5 things to consider putting in place for your flexibility.

Flexibility is much more difficult when you have the added responsibility of ensuring that your needs are met and that the new plan, environment or circumstances are accessible to you.

As an autistic ADHDer who is in the minority in most social and professional environments, it is almost always on <u>me</u> to adapt to the people around me, rather than them adapting to my needs, or even meeting me in the middle.

What is flexibility?

When we hear the word 'flexibility', we might immediately think of a gymnast doing the splits. However, when it comes to executive functioning, what we're actually talking about is something called **cognitive flexibility**. Flexibility is defined as 'the ability to adapt and adjust to changing circumstances, perspectives, or demands' and refers to the way that we need to mould and bend our behaviours, ways of working, plans of action and ways of being in order to react to the changes in the world around us.

An example of something that caused the whole world to demonstrate a huge amount of flexibility was the COVID-19 pandemic and lockdowns. Overnight, we had to change the way we worked, the way we learned, the way we socialized, the way we took care of ourselves, the way we communicated and the things we prioritized. While the pandemic forced us to be flexible on a huge scale, we're all faced with changes, however big or small, that we must adapt to every single day.

- **Maybe your train is delayed (which seems to almost always be the case if you're travelling from Manchester), so you have to plan a different route or mode of transport for your journey.**

- **Maybe someone asks you something that you weren't expecting, so you have to quickly come up with a response that you hadn't planned ahead.**

- Maybe you learn something new which takes a project you're working on in a new direction.

- Maybe the restaurant you planned to eat at doesn't have any tables available, so you have to find someplace else to eat.

- Maybe you switch from a corporate environment with your colleagues to a more relaxed, social environment with your friends, so you switch up the way you communicate in a short space of time.

Whatever those changing demands, circumstances or perspectives might be, only one thing is certain: that everything is always changing all the time. As an autistic person, I think flexibility is probably one of the executive functioning skills that causes me the most discomfort and anxiety. I don't like being caught off guard, and I don't like last-minute changes. I like things to be neatly and nicely planned out in advance, so I can run over them a hundred times in my head to make sure that everything will run smoothly. When something does change that makes my plan go off-course, it feels like the world is ending, and I think that this is down to a few different traits that fall under the autistic spectrum:

- **Literal thinking or processing**
  As literal thinkers or processors, we will often take what we are told as gospel. This means that if somebody tells us something, we will always believe it to be true – and so even if it was just a possibility or an option, if it was communicated to us, we'll think it to be

a dead cert, leaving little room for expecting things to change.

- **Black-and-white thinking**

Similarly, black-and-white or all-or-nothing thinking can lead us to see things without any room for grey. If the plan was to meet somebody at 3 p.m., and it gets to 3.05 p.m. and there is no sign of them, this feels like everything is wrong. And with that all-or-nothing thinking, we're prone to thinking that as soon as one small thing goes wrong and, therefore, the day is no longer 'perfect', it must be completely bad.

- **Repeated behaviours or routines**

Autistic people are often reliant on routines and structures to ease our anxiety and keep our nervous system regulated. For me, I think this comes from a need to feel like, in an ever-changing world, there is always at least one thing that remains constant and under my control. If these routines or repeated behaviours are affected or disrupted, this can cause a huge amount of anxiety which then leaves us feeling on edge and not in the most positive frame of mind to adapt to the change.

- **Struggles with transitioning**

Thanks to something called autistic inertia (more on this in **Tip 24: Inertia Insight**), we can struggle to transition between tasks or 'modes', making adapting to changes difficult. If we're in the flow working on one thing, and suddenly a change of circumstances means we need to jump to another task, it's tricky for our brains to first of all wind down from the 'motion' of the first task to stop, then to switch to the new task, and then to get going again with that.

- **Social rules, cues and hierarchies**
Flexibility could also refer to our ability to adapt our behaviour or communication style depending on the different circumstances or environments that we are faced with. For example, switching up the way we communicate depending on whether we are chatting with our friends in the pub or talking to our manager in a meeting. Since, as autistic people, we don't always put as much weight or importance on social hierarchies as neurotypical people do, we might not be as flexible in changing our communication styles as we don't see a need to behave any differently just because someone is more 'senior' than us in a hierarchy – whether that's subconsciously in communicating in a certain way, or making a conscious decision not to alter our communication styles. Similarly, since we're not always able to read unspoken social cues (such as body language or facial expressions), we might not notice that somebody's attitude or emotions have changed during a conversation, and so we might not be able to adapt to suit these changes.

Essentially, a lot of the autistic experience means that adapting to change without warning can be incredibly tricky, and this is also true for many other neurodivergent and disabled people. As disabled and neurodivergent people who live in a world that was never designed with our needs in mind and so often need accommodating, it isn't as easy to swap and change things quickly while making sure that these accommodations remain in place. An example of this which might help make things clearer could be that if a physically disabled wheelchair user discovers that their train is cancelled, and so needs to find another way of getting to their destination, they would need to know that the method of transport had a wheelchair space, that the station had step-free access, that there were disabled toilets on the way, and so on and so forth. Flexibility is much more difficult when you have the added responsibility of ensuring that your needs are met and that the new plan, environment or circumstances are accessible to you.

Which systems have affected the way we think about flexibility?

Flexibility allows us to adapt our behaviours, ways of working, and ways of thinking in order to suit changing circumstances; however, the biases and systems of oppression that are rife within our culture mean that it has often been skewed as to **who** needs to be flexible and in what ways. The 'norm', especially in workplaces and positions of power, has been considered to be those who hold the most privilege – cisgender, heterosexual, non-disabled, neurotypical White men – and those who fall outside of these 'norms', and therefore who are marginalized by systems of oppression, such as women and people marginalized for their gender, people of colour, queer and trans people, and disabled people, are expected to be more flexible to suit those who hold the privilege. For example, autistic and otherwise neurodivergent people are expected to mask in order to 'appear more neurotypical', queer people have often had to attempt to pass as straight or keep their queerness a secret to remain safe in straight spaces, and Black people often have to code-switch and assimilate in order to remain safe in our White supremacy culture.

This White supremacy culture, when combined with the capitalist society that we all operate under, also puts a huge weight on the amount that we are able to achieve, which Tema Okun describes as '**Progress is Bigger/More**' in her White supremacy culture characteristics. **Progress is Bigger/More** explains the way that we, as a capitalist society, always seem to be striving for more, bigger, or better. We define success as having more money, more employees, a bigger house, more cars, more holidays, etc., when, in reality, that might not feel like success to many people. This way of thinking does not allow for the fact that people might have their own personal definitions of progress or success, and that progress might be non-linear or less visible from an outside perspective. It also does not account for the cost that comes with progress – for example, I might be seen as more and more 'successful' as I gain more followers on social media, but there is no consideration of the fact that this means that I might be under more pressure, might have to commit more time to the work, or might not be able to enjoy certain spaces in the same way any more. (This is, obviously, an incredibly privileged example – it is just the first thing that sprang to mind!) Defining progress as 'bigger' or 'more' also causes us to value those who have 'progressed' over those who haven't; for example, those who have climbed up the corporate ladder, built a large business, bought expensive houses or gained multiple degrees.

How Progress is Bigger/More affects the way we see flexibility and executive functioning:

- An emphasis on 'Bigger/More' creates an environment with constant pressure to achieve and earn more, work faster and juggle more plates, which means that the executive functioning skill of flexibility is deemed to have huge significance. Since we are always striving to achieve more and work at a faster pace, we're faced with more changes and challenges to overcome, and are expected to overcome or adapt to them at a much faster pace. This added significance is also placed on some of our other executive functioning skills, such as task initiation, prioritization, planning and organization.

- Additionally, we are constantly encouraged to add more to our plate, take on more projects, or do more complicated things, instead of being able to focus on maintaining our current levels of functioning and increasing our happiness and confidence. This means we're constantly having to be flexible in switching between all these tasks or projects, rather than being content focusing on one thing at a time and doing it well.

- This mindset can set unrealistic expectations of progress or success, causing frustration, stress, and a sense of failure if you cannot meet these incredibly high standards.

Additionally, in patriarchal, heteronormative relationships and marriages, women are generally still expected to take on unpaid roles as 'homemakers', which often includes taking on the majority of child-care responsibilities. This requires a great deal of flexibility, as looking after a young baby who can only communicate their needs by crying is perhaps one of the environments which requires us to adapt the most! A mother might think a baby is crying because they are hungry, and therefore go to feed them, but then find that they are not inter-ested in their bottle, and so have to adapt and problem solve to work out what it is that their child is trying to communicate and therefore how to meet their needs. Then, as the child grows older, mothers are often required to stop what they are doing at the drop of a hat in order to meet the child's needs: whether this is rushing from work to pick them up from school if they are unwell, stopping what they are doing in order to comfort the child if they are upset, or interrupting their evening routine if the child is unable to sleep. Life becomes even more unpredictable when you have a whole other human to take care of, which requires an even greater deal of flexibility to work around.

Finally, as touched on above, I believe that the ableism and neuro-normativity that are present throughout our society mean that neurodivergent and disabled people are required to be dispropor-tionately flexible compared to their neurotypical or non-disabled counterparts. As an autistic ADHDer who is in the minority in most social and professional environments, it is almost always on **me** to adapt to the people around me, rather than them adapting to my needs, or even meeting me in the middle. I don't pick up on the same clues, whether that's facial expressions or non-verbal commu-nication, and I can't read between the lines like the other people in the room, so I am having to navigate situations and conversations with a huge amount of missing context. This, tied with the ostraciza-tion and exclusion that most of us have faced throughout our lives, means that we are often hypervigilant and 'walking on eggshells' to adapt and change our tone of voice, communication styles, facial expressions, body language and overall ways of being in order to stop things from going off-course. This requires a huge amount of flexibility – a skill which we know is already delayed or affected in neurodivergent people – and so it is no surprise that our capacity to adapt to other circumstances or changes might be depleted.

How can we support ourselves with flexibility?

As with all the executive functioning skills that we'll be exploring throughout the book, flexibility is a hugely important and necessary skill. As much as I'd like it to be otherwise, the world around us is always changing, and will continue to change for as long as it exists. This happens both on the macro level, like cultural changes as we move towards a more inclusive and accessible society, and on the micro level, like having to adapt your plans last-minute thanks to a change in the weather, and can be both positive and negative, or a combination of the two. Change is inevitable, and we are always going to have to be able to adapt to it; that is human nature.

However, as we have explored above, many of the expectations placed on marginalized people to be flexible, and adapt their ways of working, thinking, communicating and being, are impacted by the systems of oppression and biases in our society. Yes, we will always have to adapt to changes, but we should never have to adapt **who we are** in order to be accepted, included or safe. As I have often said when I've felt deflated after having to leave an environment because of sensory overload causing a meltdown or shutdown, this is **never** a personal failing on your part, it is an accessibility failing on the part of the venue or event organizer. Obviously, the world we live in is far from perfect, and it is often necessary for those of us who are marginalized by multiple systems of oppression to adapt and change our behaviours to remain safe – and this is especially true of Black people, people of colour, and trans people – however, I am hopeful that, over time, we will see a more inclusive and accepting society which allows us to let go of the expectation that we have to adapt who we are depending on our surroundings.

I am also a big believer that being inflexible in certain situations gives us more capacity to be flexible in others. We are faced with a huge number of changes, challenges and decisions every single day, which can be incredibly overwhelming, but by maintaining consistency across certain situations and decisions, we ease off some of the pressure that is constantly applied to our cognitive flexibility. One example of this is the infamous 'Steve Jobs uniform'. Steve Jobs, the late co-founder and CEO of Apple, became notorious for wearing the same signature look every day: a black turtleneck, blue jeans, and a pair of New Balance trainers. He would wear this same combination of clothes each day, no matter where he was going, what he was doing, or who he was meeting. It is claimed that his reasoning for doing so was that he knew that the less time he made making mundane decisions (like about what to wear), the more time, energy and capacity he had for the things that were more important to him – like bigger decisions and creativity. In a 2012 interview with *Vanity Fair*, Barack Obama, then President of the USA, explained his reasoning behind making a similar decision:

You'll see I wear only gray or blue suits. I'm trying
to pare down decisions. I don't want to make
decisions about what I'm eating or wearing.
Because I have too many other decisions to make.
You need to focus your decision-making energy.
You need to routinize yourself. You can't be going
through the day distracted by trivia.

Essentially, flexibility is a necessary skill, but that does not mean it is necessary (or even a good idea) for us to be flexible about everything all the time. If maintaining rigidity, consistency and reliability in certain aspects of your life eases your anxiety, feels more comfortable and requires less energy, then that is a perfectly okay thing to do. Like all our executive functioning skills, it's about finding the balance of which expectations and norms we can let go of, and which are the times that flexibility is truly necessary – and then finding ways of supporting ourselves through those situations.

The best way that I have found to support myself with being flexible in times of change and turbulence is to be inflexible and rigid in the things that are under my control, and therefore maintaining some level of consistency and safety throughout the change. This might look like:

- Sticking to the same morning routine every day, no matter what your plans for the day are.

- Having the same breakfast every morning.

- Sticking to the same bedtime every night.

- Taking your own pillow when you go on holiday.

- Having your same non-negotiables scheduled in, like going for a walk or reading before bed even when the rest of your schedule is all over the place.

- Listening to the same songs on repeat throughout times of change.

- Locating a safe food at a fast food chain that's widely available across the globe (I know I can get my McNuggets fix if I'm feeling low whether I'm at home in Manchester, in London for work, or abroad on holiday).

A list of things that are <u>absolutely fine</u>:

- Sticking to a routine that suits you and asking other people and their demands to work around that, rather than you always having to work around them.

- Needing a little bit of extra time to get used to changes or switch between different tasks.

- Saying 'no' to something you previously said 'yes' to if the expectations or demands change and would have influenced your decision had you known that information to start off with.

- Having non-negotiable rules such as only being able to travel if you have three days' notice, or needing an agenda within a certain amount of time before a meeting.

- Admitting that you were previously wrong, and updating your views, thoughts or beliefs as you learn (this one is a very tricky one, I know!).

- Doing things a certain way or following certain routines if doing so eases your anxiety or makes you feel better, even if these things don't make sense to other people.

- Showing up as yourself in different environments – whether that's wearing what you feel most comfortable in, not wearing make-up when you might be expected to, or communicating in the same way no matter who you're communicating with.

- Eating the same things every day or wearing the same clothes every day (or buying multiples of the same item of clothing so you can keep on wearing it even when one is in the wash!).

- Needing to go over things or process things verbally when something changes to be able to get your head around it.

- Asking for extra information about a change before agreeing to it or going ahead.

Tip 21:
Energy rating

By Charlie Rewilding (she/her), autistic and ADHD content creator and writer

My energy fluctuates day to day, I struggle to intuitively predict how long tasks will take me, and I often find it difficult to take breaks and shift between tasks. This makes day-to-day life **stressful and challenging**. Before I understood my brain, I internalized these challenges and felt like I was stupid – but now that I understand my brain better, I use certain tactics that help make daily tasks more accessible to me while simultaneously managing my energy levels.

For example, I realized that traditional to-do lists don't help me with day-to-day living – but there are a few ways I can adapt my to-do lists to make it more likely that I complete the tasks I have while mitigating my risk of burning out. My main consideration now is not how much I can get done in a specific period of **time** – but instead how much **energy** I have available to allocate between tasks.

I colour-code my to-do list with:

- **Green:** meaning 'this task will take minimal energy'.

- **Yellow:** meaning 'this task will take a fair amount of energy'.

- **Red:** meaning 'this task will take a lot of energy'.

Depending on the energy I have for a given day, I use this visual colour-coded system to help me prioritize tasks or shift them to another day. For example, I might focus on green-coded tasks on days when I'm lacking energy because I have been faced with a last-minute change to my plans. Or, if I wake up with more energy than I was anticipating, I might choose to tackle the red-coded tasks first. Having this colour-coded system allows me to adjust to changing circumstances and demands while reminding me to prioritize my needs and feel accomplished in completing daily tasks.

You can write out your to-do list in this table, with space to colour-code each task by how much energy it will take. Feel free to copy the table out into your own notebook or planner if you need more space!

To do	Energy rating

Tip 22:
Four quadrants

As a perfectionist and black-and-white thinker (thanks to being an autistic ADHDer), I often struggle with feeling as though if one thing has gone wrong, that's the whole day written off as a bad one. Didn't start working at exactly 9:00 on the dot? Well then, I've failed, and it's going to be a rubbish day. Haven't had a productive morning? Well then, I may as well give up for the day. I personally do work best first thing in the morning because if I don't start the day in work mode, I struggle to transition into it later on (more on this later in the chapter), but there is one really handy tip that can help you work around that all-or-nothing thinking.

Instead of thinking about your day as one long day, you can split it into four quadrants:

- **Quadrant 1 – morning** - 8 a.m. to 11 a.m.

- **Quadrant 2 – lunch** - 11 a.m. to 2 p.m.

- **Quadrant 3 – afternoon** - 2 p.m. to 5 p.m.

- **Quadrant 4 – evening** - 5 p.m. to 8 p.m.

Feel free to shift the timings either way if you're more of an early bird or a night owl; it's the concept of splitting it into four chunks that matters. Then, when planning out your day, you're going to assign tasks, to-dos, or activities to a specific quadrant.

That way, if, for example, your morning quadrant feels completely unproductive – not to worry! You have three more chances to start again from scratch. It's no longer the case that the whole day is ruined or the whole day is going to be unproductive; it was simply a bad quadrant.

There is nothing ground-breaking about this tip – but sometimes it is the simplest reframing that helps us the most. We know that we're prone to thinking about thinking in a very all-or-nothing, black-and-white way, so we can work around that by putting these boundaries into place. Opposite, you'll find an example of a four-quadrant template to split your day with.

Bonus tip: Try to stick to one main activity per quadrant if you can (for example, clump together all admin tasks into one quadrant). Task-switching can be difficult for busy brains – and, regardless of neurotype, jumping between lots of different tasks most likely isn't going to be the most productive way of working.

Quadrant 1	**Quadrant 2**
Self-care	Admin tasks
— Shower	— Catch up on emails
— Eat breakfast	— Complete quick ticks
— Get dressed	— Order prescription
— Do hair	— Post social media post
— Do make-up	— Plan content for next week
— Plan for day	— _____
— _____	— _____
— _____	— _____
— _____	— _____
— _____	— _____

Quadrant 3	**Quadrant 4**
Creative tasks	Debrief and unwind
— Record video	— Update to-do's with what I've
— Edit video	managed to get done
— Design cover thumbnail for	— Check through calendar for
video	tomorrow to make sure I'm
— _____	prepared
— _____	— Switch off by going for a walk
— _____	— Make dinner
— _____	— _____
— _____	— _____
— _____	— _____
— _____	— _____

Tip 23:
Winning with waiting mode

One of the things that makes it tricky for me to be flexible is something called **waiting mode** – a term coined by the ADHD community to explain the frame of mind they often get stuck in when they know they have something coming up later on in the day, and therefore can't get anything done beforehand. If, for example, I know I have an appointment at 2 p.m., the whole day beforehand I'm stuck in 'waiting mode', counting the seconds until 2 p.m. comes around. For me, I think this comes from a few different places:

1. **Working memory**
   As we discussed in **Chapter 1: Working memory (page 57)**, neurodivergent folks can often struggle to juggle as many things at once because of their differences in working memory capacity. If we use that 2 p.m. appointment as an example, for me, I know that if I stop thinking about it for a second, it would be so easy for me to forget about it because of all the other stuff that's flying around my brain at any one time. So instead, I cling on to thinking about it to make sure I don't miss it.

2. **Hyperfocus**
   Similarly, with a brain that's prone to hyperfocusing, it would be easy to completely miss an appointment.

Hyperfocus refers to a really intense state of focus, fixation or interest in a certain activity for an extended period. It can be explained as a more intense version of a neurotypical 'flow' state or feeling of being 'in the zone'. You become so engrossed in the task at hand that you almost forget the rest of the world around you exists – including any appointments that might be scheduled in for that time.

3. Time blindness

Many ADHDers also experience time blindness, which explains the way that we tend to think of time as 'now' or 'not now', and find it difficult to judge how long something might take, or how much time has passed – especially if we're in one of those hyperfocus states mentioned above. For this reason, it can be tricky for us to work out what we'd be able to get done between now and our 2 p.m. appointment, because we have no gauge for what that length of time feels like, leaving us stuck in waiting mode.

4. Decision freeze

Decision freeze, also frequently known as decision paralysis, explains the way that neurodivergent people (ADHDers and autistic people, especially) may become overwhelmed when there are too many decisions at hand and therefore not be able to make any decision at all. For me, this feels like my brain is unable to compute all the different choices, and the pros and cons for each of those choices, and sort of flashes up an imaginary 'Error 404' message. When we know we have a certain amount of time to fill before our 2 p.m. appointment, the options of what we could do in that time period might feel endless. On top of this, deciding which order to do those tasks in can make it even trickier – for example, say I have a 2 p.m. appointment that I need to get to, my morning thought process usually goes something like this:

I need to shower. But I want to go to the gym at some point today, so there's no point in showering before I go to the gym. So I should shower first. But I need to eat before I go to the gym. So I should eat first, and then gym, and then shower. But I'll need to wait some time between eating and going to the gym. So do I have time to go to the gym? If I eat, that might take about ten minutes, and then I might need an hour to let my food settle, and then it's ten minutes to go to the gym. And then how long do I usually spend in the gym? Maybe about an hour? And then I can shower, does that take about twenty minutes? And then I need ten minutes to get back. But I know that I usually get distracted so I probably need to allow an extra hour in total to make sure I'm not late for the appointment. Actually I think my car probably needs some petrol before I set off, so how far out of my way is that? And how long will it take me to get to the appointment? So do I have time for all of that?

And then because I've spent so much time going backwards and forwards about all the different options and ideas, my brain becomes incredibly overwhelmed and decides, actually, we won't do any of it, and I just get stuck in waiting mode until the appointment.

Although it's easy to understand **why** waiting mode comes about, it can still be incredibly annoying sometimes. It wastes big chunks of time when you could be getting on with something important, and also can just feel torturous when you're an impatient, impulsive ADHDer. However, I've found a few ways that you can beat waiting mode:

- Where possible, schedule all meetings and appointments as early as you can. That way, you can get them out of the way first thing in the morning, and then have the rest of the day to do what you please, instead of waiting around for an afternoon appointment.

- Start recording and making a list of how long certain tasks generally take you. That way, you know exactly which you can and can't fit into the time between now and your appointment, without having to get stuck in the chaotic cycle of thoughts we went through above. You can find some space to do this on the following page.

- If you do have any appointments in the afternoon, set alarms or reminders for them on your phone or home assistant (e.g. Siri or Alexa). If you set a reminder for, say, ten minutes before the start time of the appointment or before you need to leave the house, you know that, no matter how engrossed you get in a task, you still won't miss your appointment later.

Task	How long it takes

Tip 24:
Inertia insight

Another thing that can make being flexible tricky is **autistic inertia**. To understand what autistic inertia is, it's helpful to start by defining what 'actual' inertia is. In physics, inertia explains the tendency of objects to stay in their current state. Objects that are already in motion will stay in motion, and objects that are at rest will stay at rest, unless an external force causes their speed or direction to change. Hypothetically, if you were to push an object in a perfect vacuum without any gravity, friction or air resistance to slow it down, that object would continue to move forever in the same direction. Similarly, an object that is still will never move unless acted upon by an outside force.

Once we understand inertia, we can put this into the context of autistic inertia. Autistic inertia is the tendency that autistic people have to want to remain in a constant state. As Quincy Hansen explains in their blog Speaking of Autism:

> When we're asleep we want to stay asleep, when awake we want to stay awake, when we're working on one thing we want to keep working on it, when we're doing one thing we want to keep doing that one thing, etc. Now, yes, this tendency exists in everybody but you must understand that this is

often significantly more pronounced in autistic people.

This explains the way that it can be really tricky for us to go from not doing anything to starting a task (more on this in **Chapter 7: Task initiation, page 267**), and similarly, once we get into our flow with a task, it can be really hard for us to stop, or switch to another task. This might explain the way that you say 'just one minute' when someone asks you to stop what you're doing, because it's hard to force your brain to a hard stop. And quite often even neurotypical people can accidentally keep doing it for another long while. Imagine that feeling but on every task, hobby and action throughout every day.

This concept of autistic inertia can be applied on a more macro scale, too. For example, when I am going through a really busy period of time, even if I know that I need to rest, it can be really hard for me to transition out of my state of busyness. And once I do manage to stop, for example when everything winds down around Christmas and New Year time, it can be really tricky to get back into the swing of things again.

Autistic inertia is something that I really struggle with personally, and when researching tips to include in this book, I came across a suggestion on Reddit (from user TimorousAlice) that made me audibly gasp because of how genius it was, and I knew I needed to include it to share with you.

To help with autistic inertia when switching between tasks (or states), you need to find something that can stay constant across both states.

TimorousAlice gave the example of playing an audiobook, and explained, 'I put on the audiobook on my phone while doing task A, and keep listening while I start task B. It gives me a little bit of consistency between the two tasks, softening the transition a little.'

You could also replicate this with:

- Putting the same song or album on repeat.

- Listening to a podcast.

- Playing with a fidget toy that you continue to play with when you shift tasks.

- Starting a phone call during task A, which you continue through to task B.

The idea is to keep something constant between the two tasks, so that, while you are still transitioning, some of your experience is staying constant. This way, your brain isn't as aware of the fact that it's being made to transition!

Tip 25:
Trial run

By Neurodivergent Lou (she/her), autistic content creator

Being autistic feels like navigating a world where everyone else holds a secret rule book, guiding them effortlessly through the nuances of daily life. A rule book that tells them what to do, how to be, and the expected sequence of events. Yet, for some reason, as neurodivergent people, it can feel like we are missing this shared rule book, navigating in darkness.

This feeling of unpredictability becomes particularly amplified when visiting new places for the first time. **Autistic brains process on average 42% more information at rest** and processing information about new environments can be even more demanding. Combine this with amplified sensory input, a change in routine and emotional regulation struggles, and there is potential for disaster – such as meltdowns, shutdowns or feeling very overwhelmed.

Yet one way that I have found to consistently avoid being thrown by new places is by using **Google Earth Street View** to virtually 'walk through' the route before I do it. It allows me to view exactly what the place will look like in advance. I now don't go anywhere new without seeing the place or virtually 'walking' the route, whether I am going to a supermarket, office, a hospital appointment or the train station. Throughout my life as a neurodivergent human, I have tried and tested many strategies to create predictability, but this is the one I always come back to.

It gives me a chance to work with the detail-orientated nature of my brain, rather than working against it. To have the opportunity to process the environment, in my own time and space, before I am fully immersed in it. It turns what feels like an out-of-control situation into a situation that is manageable; it makes the unpredictable feel predictable. It creates a concrete visual reference rather than relying on an abstract idea in my head. For autistic people, imagining what a place looks like without a visual reference can be impossible. Looking at places and routes in advance can help to regulate emotions too, reducing the potential anxiety and distress associated with new environments.

Not only does it help with processing the environment, but using Street View can help us to recognize potential triggers in a new environment too. It lets us prepare for, anticipate and mitigate these challenges. For example, recognizing where an environment might be really busy and difficult to navigate or where sensory overload may be triggered. It empowers us to be able to accommodate ourselves, whether that is by using noise-cancelling headphones to reduce the layers of noise in the environment or travelling an alternative route.

Flexibility recap

Our fifth executive functioning skill, **flexibility**, describes our ability to switch between tasks and demands in response to changes in the environment. It is the skill which allows us to adapt and change our behaviour depending on different contexts or stimuli in our world. In an ever-changing world, flexibility is one of the most important skills, allowing us to stay safe, adapt to our surroundings, problem solve, move between different tasks, and keep up with the changing demands that are placed on us.

However, as with all the executive functioning skills we have explored so far, the ways that we are currently expected to adapt and change rely on us compromising on (or even completely moving away from) our brain's natural ways of thinking, working and being. While flexibility has its benefits, sometimes remaining rigid around our routines, decisions and structures frees up the brain space that we need to focus on the big decisions and changes, while reducing anxiety and leaving our nervous systems feeling regulated.

In this chapter, we have explored:

- **What flexibility is.**
- **The systems which have affected the way we think about flexibility.**
- **Some ways we can support ourselves with flexibility.**
- **5 things to consider putting in place for your flexibility.**

Your takeaway box

- Flexibility is vital in being able to adapt according to changing circumstances, but you should never be expected to change **who you are** as a person in order to feel included, safe or accepted. Changing the way that you think about things or problem solving to work around a change of plans are necessary ways of keeping up with the world around you, but that shouldn't require you to be flexible on your non-negotiables, your values, or the ways of being that come naturally to you as a neurodivergent person.

- By remaining rigid in some areas of life, for example, by following routines, having structures in place and standardizing certain decisions, we free up the brain space we need to be able to be flexible in other, more important or necessary areas. It's okay to wear the same clothes, eat the same food, or follow the same morning routine every day if that is what makes you feel the most comfortable!

- By being aware of our own thought patterns and the changes that generally feel most difficult for us, we can support ourselves to feel more comfortable throughout changing circumstances that might otherwise be overwhelming or anxiety-inducing. We cannot exactly predict the problems that we're going to face each day or the things that are going to throw us off plan, but we can prepare ourselves with a plan B, or tools that help us feel calmer throughout these changes.

6

Planning and prioritization

As someone who is both autistic and ADHD, I feel like I oscillate between two extremes: having everything planned out months in advance right down to the tiniest details, or spontaneously jumping into things with no planning whatsoever. Sometimes, I can find such joy in researching a trip, for example, and planning out all the travel details, timings, connection routes, accommodation locations, agendas and itineraries right down to where I want to eat each day, and other times the thought of planning out how I'm going to complete a big project feels so overwhelming that it can bring me to tears.

When tasked with a big project like writing this book, for example, the big-picture end result feels incredibly exciting. But then trying to work out how to break it down into each step and plan out the structure and prioritize which information needs to go inside and how much I should write about each topic, and which are the most important key points that I want to focus on and how long it's going to take me to write and when I'm going to fit the writing in between the other things I've got going on and on and on and on feels incredibly overwhelming and anxiety-inducing, like my brain is an ancient computer that's going to overheat and start smoking from the sides as it tries to solve a hundred different problems all at once. If you relate to any of the above, then it's likely that planning and prioritization is something that you have differences with, too, and we'll explore ways to support ourselves later in the chapter.

In this chapter, we will explore:

- What is planning and prioritization?

- Which systems have affected the way we think about planning and prioritization?

- How can we support ourselves with planning and prioritization?

- 5 things to consider putting in place for your planning and prioritization.

Often, when people say that 'autistic people struggle with prioritization', what they actually mean is that we don't always prioritize the things that **they** want us to prioritize in the ways that **they** want us to prioritize them.

Research has shown that autistic brains generate and process on average <u>42% more information at rest</u>, and with all that extra information, it is no wonder that it can be trickier for us to filter through it in order to plan and prioritize.

What is planning and prioritization?

Planning and prioritization is defined as the ability to create a systematic approach to achieving goals, including breaking tasks into steps and determining their relative importance. Rather than being a single, stand-alone executive functioning skill, it actually also requires a whole range of the other skills we've explored, such as working memory (keeping track of all the different steps of a task at once) and flexibility (considering different options for the different steps involved). Neurodivergent people, especially those who are autistic, ADHD or dyslexic, tend to lean towards **big-picture thinking**, which means that we can very easily imagine the end goal that we want to achieve, but the attention to detail and prioritization required to actually break that goal down into each small step that is required, and in which order those steps are required to take place, can be tricky for us.

One explanation for this in autistic people is something known as **bottom-up processing** (or thinking), which is one of my very favourite parts of the autistic experience to speak, write and learn about, and which I dug into in my first book, *unmasked*. Bottom-up processing comes from the theory that there are two distinct ways in which humans process information. Most neurotypical people tend to process information in what is known as a 'top-down' way, which means that, when they are faced with a situation, they will start from the top, seeing the situation or 'picture' as a whole, and work downwards. They already have their previous experiences and understandings stored away in their mind, and they will use this context to help them build out this big picture. From there, they will work downwards, and seek out any further pieces of information that they need as and when they need them. For example, if they were to walk into a restaurant, they would think, 'Oh, okay, we're in a restaurant! I have been to many restaurants before, and so I understand the gist of the situation that I'm in.' Then, they would pick out pieces of information as they needed them – such as listening to the person sitting across the table from them, reading the section of the menu that they were interested in, or looking for the 'Toilets' sign when they needed to go.

For the most part, though, they'd be filtering out the majority of the stuff going on in the room that wasn't necessary for them. They'd be filtering out the conversations that other people were having on the tables around them, the smells of all the different dishes, and the bright lights coming from the ceiling. They start at the top, the context, and work downwards to fill in the details of the situation that they need.

However, for those of us who are bottom-up processors, which is usually the case for autistic people, the opposite happens. If we were to walk into that same restaurant, we would process the information in a completely different way. Rather than starting with the context, we start from zero, and take in all the sensory information around us to build up to that big picture. We'd start at the bottom, and take in all the different sounds (the squeaky chairs, the clashing conversations, the pots and pans banging in the kitchen, and the music playing in the background), all the visual stimuli (the different dishes being carried to the tables, the specials board on the wall, the signs for the toilets, and the people on each of the tables), and the different smells (from the different dishes on different tables and the cooking in the kitchen). We would piece together all these bits of information, working from the bottom upwards, to eventually work out, 'Ah! We are in a restaurant! And I now know this individual restaurant very well!' **We start from the bottom, process the information brick-by-brick, and piece it together to build the whole picture.**

Our brains need to collect **all** the information around us in order to process and piece together what is going on, which means that first, it is not prioritizing the information from the beginning because it needs **all** of it to get started. Second, once all that information has come in together, it becomes incredibly difficult to further prioritize from such a vast array of individual items. A bottom-up processor is like a huge lorry tipping and pouring out hundreds of books all around you and trying to work out which were the most interesting to you, as opposed to a top-down processor walking into a library and easily locating the one book that they wanted.

As mentioned earlier, research has shown that autistic brains generate and process, on average, **42% more information at rest**, and with all that extra information (like all the books from the lorry), it is no wonder that it can be trickier for us to filter through it in order to plan and prioritize. I would imagine that the same is also true for ADHDers; with brains that are constantly seeking out and searching for our next source of stimulation, and internal hyperactivity that is bouncing around hundreds of thoughts at any given moment, we must have much more information to filter through, plan and prioritize than our neurotypical peers.

Which systems have affected the way we think about planning and prioritization?

The ways that we are expected to plan and prioritize have, of course, been impacted by what is deemed 'normal' and important within our society. I think the biggest example of this is that under capitalism, we are expected to prioritize productivity, work and our careers above all else. For most people, their jobs (whether employed or self-employed) have to come before all else from 9 a.m. until 5 p.m., five days a week. Often where we decide to live, who we build relationships with, the hobbies that we are able to take part in, and the vast majority of the decisions that we make, are influenced by doing 'what is best' for our career, i.e. capitalism. Even in extreme circumstances, like when a family have a new baby, or when we experience loss and grief, it is only for an incredibly short amount of time that we are expected to shift our priority away from work. Maybe you're only allowed a couple of days of compassionate leave or a couple of weeks of parental leave, and after that, you are expected to jump right back to your job being your main priority for the majority of your day, no matter what else you have going on in your life.

Although I know that I objectively have a hard time knowing which tasks are more important for me to start with, which information is most important for me to share, and what needs to be done for me to get to where I want to be, I also believe that, often, when people say that 'autistic people struggle with prioritization', what they actually mean is that we don't always prioritize the things that **they** want us to prioritize in the ways that **they** want us to prioritize them. Since we often place less emphasis on social norms and hierarchies, and are more likely to think independently than follow the things that society tells us we 'should' do, we might also be more likely to prioritize what *actually* feels more important to us, rather than what we've been told we 'should' prioritize.

Yes, I can struggle to work out which information is the most important to relay.

But also . . . **maybe I just personally find it more important to infodump about something I love than to talk about the weather?**

Yes, I can struggle to know which tasks are more important for me to complete first.

But also . . . **maybe I just don't think that emails should take priority over something that's going to make me feel good?**

Yes, I can struggle with planning out how to keep on top of my home around working full-time.

But also . . . **maybe I just don't feel like humans were designed to do a job for forty hours a week and then come home and complete all the labour that running a household requires?**

As individual, unique human beings, we will all, naturally, have different priorities, but the way that we currently work and live under capitalism forces us into a box where our main priority is making money. Not only that, conforming to this structure keeps the power in the hands of those who currently hold it. If things get in the way of our ability to be productive (aka make money), we are told that we have prioritized 'incorrectly'. However, if we didn't live in such a capitalist society, there would be no 'right' or 'wrong' thing to prioritize, just the priorities that mattered most to us. The same concept applies to gender norms that are imposed upon women to 'prioritize starting a family'; and heteronormative, monogamous relationship expectations, which assume we will pick one person or partner that we prioritize over the rest. If these societal norms and expectations weren't seen as the only 'right' way to do things, there would be no issue with our decision to prioritize different things.

Additionally, under White supremacy culture, Tema Okun describes the way that we have prioritized certain ways of communicating, in what she describes as **worship of the written word**. In White supremacy culture, we value things that are written down over any other form of communication. As an example which will be relatable for many of us, let's consider trying to access a medical diagnosis of autism or ADHD. In order to access any support, we have to fill out endless forms and communicate our needs and experiences in a written format. For our experiences to 'matter' or 'exist', they must be written or printed in black and white on a sheet of paper. Paper trails and written words are seen as the only or most legitimate source of information, and we don't account for the way that many cultures have passed on valuable knowledge and stories verbally for thousands of years, and that those stories or pieces of information are just as valid as others that happen to be written down.

I also find that this shows up in our insistence that the only way to become an 'expert' is via academia; those who are university-educated and have both studied the written word, and shared their own research via the written word, are seen as more 'legitimate' or 'qualified' than, for example, somebody who has lived experience, or has learned by seeing and listening to a certain community or person, or by picking skills up from the people around them. I am almost definitely seen as more 'legitimate' or 'professional' now that I am a published author than when I was 'just' a content creator, even though the information and thoughts that I was sharing in the videos I was creating came from the exact same person and had the exact same value (and often exact same content!) as what was in the book. See also how, when sharing some new information with a friend or colleague, you might feel you have to tell them that you 'read an article' about it recently when, actually, you learned it from a video on TikTok – because an article (written word) is valued much more highly even when the same information is being shared. Facts are facts – whether they are communicated verbally or in a written article, they still hold the same value and importance!

How worship of the written word affects the way we see planning, prioritization and executive functioning:

- In our current academic and education systems there is a disproportionate amount of value placed on the written word and therefore our ability to read, write and study 'effectively'. These traditional methods of studying, revising or researching using written materials might require more of our executive functioning capabilities than if we just had to remember information communicated to us verbally, for example. If we valued other forms of communicating information as just as valid as the written word, the academic world would be more accessible to the neurodivergent community.

- Those who struggle with executive functioning may find tasks that heavily rely on written expression or documentation more difficult, which might lead to their competence being misinterpreted or underestimated. Their challenges in organizing thoughts, planning or prioritizing ideas **in writing** could be mistaken for a lack of intelligence or ability. Maybe it is not that you struggle to plan, but just that you find it best to do so internally or in a more abstract way, rather than writing out a to-do list. And maybe it's not that you find it difficult to prioritize information, but just that you would rather share it verbally or in a non-linear way, rather than write a report or story from start to finish.

- Our society and systems frequently rely on written forms being completed and things being written down, which means that anyone who struggles with those things misses out on many opportunities. For example, during the job application process, whether you are actually able to do the job is irrelevant if you are unable to complete the written form to apply.

How can we support ourselves with planning and prioritization?

When it comes to planning and prioritization, although there are things that we can do to support ourselves with any struggles that we have, a lot of it comes down to the fact that our brains simply work in a different way, and so we require more information and support from the people around us. With bottom-up processing, our brains are literally processing information in a completely different way than the other people around us, and than the way the world has been designed to accommodate. We cannot change our innate ways of thinking and processing, and, perhaps, we just need the world around us to instead adapt to suit our needs better. We are disabled, and, under the social model of disability, we know that that means that we are disabled **by the world around us**.

Planning and prioritization in work and in life generally would be much less difficult if we weren't expected to read between the lines and follow unwritten rules, and instead were given clear and specific instructions as to what we needed to do, what order we needed to do it in, when we needed to do it by, what the most important outcomes were, and why we needed to do it. If somebody gives you a vague instruction to 'complete XYZ project' and you aren't clear on what they want, it is not your responsibility to decipher their expectations and priorities in order to plan how to approach it. It is also perfectly acceptable to go back and ask them clarifying questions in order to work out how you will move forward. A lot of the time when I feel lost, overwhelmed and unsure where to start with a project, it is simply down to the fact that I have not been given enough information, and so my brain is working overtime to try and fill in the gaps it needs to be able to make the decisions it needs in order to move forward. I imagine it as being like a maze where one of the pathways is missing, and so the bits of information inside are going round and round in circles, trying to find the correct path, but there is no path there to follow. However, if the information that I needed to be able to plan and prioritize was simply given to me, that pathway in the maze would become clear, and the information would be able to progress through the circuit.

Essentially, what I'm trying to get across here is that yes, you can do things to adapt and support yourself with planning and prioritization, but that it is not **solely** on you; it's also on your managers to give clearer direction, your family to be specific with their requests, and your partners to support you in working out where your priorities lie.

A list of things that are <u>absolutely fine</u>:

- Prioritizing the things that matter to you, even if they don't align with the things that other people think are the most important.

- Info-dumping about your special interest because that feels like a more important thing to speak about than making small talk about the weather.

- Planning things out ahead of time to create a detailed schedule or itinerary if that eases your anxiety.

- Needing to speak things through with somebody verbally and get their outside input to work out how to plan and prioritize them.

- Asking for clarification of what should be prioritized when working on a task or project.

- Using AI (such as Tiimo or ChatGPT) to break down big tasks into smaller chunks to help you plan and prioritize which order to do them in.

- Doing things in a different order than what other people might think is 'logical' because that is the order that works best for you.

- Needing clear and specific instructions for each part of a task or project rather than being told the final output and being expected to work out each step yourself.

- Needing to reassess your plans and goals on a regular basis because you find it tricky to think about things that are a long way off.

- Focusing on one step of a project at a time rather than having the whole thing planned out right from the start.

- Adapting your priorities based on the circumstances.

Tip 26:
Big Brain Dump

If I wake up in the morning without having my day planned out, it can quickly descend into chaos. With no set time to get up and out of the house, I can spend hours lost in my tiny dopamine-machine rectangle (otherwise known as my phone), and without knowing exactly what I need to do, I can become quickly overwhelmed. If my day is left wide open, both decision freeze (more on this in **Tip 23: Winning with waiting mode, page 224**) and autistic inertia (struggling to transition from a rest state to a 'go state' – more on this in **Tip 24: Inertia insight, page 229**) can take over.

One way that I combat this is by planning out my to-do list in advance – I call this my Sunday **Big Brain Dump**. On a Sunday afternoon, I will sit down with a big A3 piece of paper and dump everything that needs to get done the following week out of my brain and on to the page. I'll include any appointments I have, any tasks I need to complete, how many gym sessions I'd like to squeeze in, and if I have any plans with friends; if it needs to get done, it's going on the paper. Then, once I have a clear view of everything that is in store for the entire week, I can pull out the tasks that I'll be able to get done the following day (Monday).

I can plan out my day with rough timings, clumping together similar tasks and working out which order it makes the most sense to do things in. (I obviously have a bit more flexibility than most people as someone who is self-employed and lives alone, but even if you have your 9 to 5 already blocked out, you can use this to manage which actual tasks you'll get done each day, and what you want to do with your free time in the morning or evening.) I'll circle them on my Big Brain Dump and then move them over to my to-do list for Monday.

Then, on Monday evening, once I've got the tasks for that day ticked off, I can come back to my Big Brain Dump. First, I'll go through the tasks that I'd circled for Monday and cross them off the master list, so I know that they've been done. Then, I can start the process again for the following day. I'll pick out the tasks for Tuesday, circle them, move them over to my Tuesday to-do list and work out the order and timings of getting them done.

I can repeat this process every night, always coming back to my Big Brain Dump and using this to schedule the following day's to-do list. Doing this means I'm making sure that all the week's tasks are getting done and that I have my day planned out ahead of time to prevent not knowing where to get started. It also has the added benefit of meaning that I know what's going on before I go to bed, so I'm not tossing and turning while my busy brain thinks about what I need to do in the morning – it's already been decided.

Tip 27:
Visual aids

One of the most common ways that parents and carers of autistic children are advised to accommodate them is by using visual schedules to let them know what to expect. Research has found that autistic people may be more responsive when information is presented visually in a step-by-step manner than when it is presented in an auditory manner.

My mum was a primary school teacher when I was younger, and when we were first exploring my suspected autism, something that she mentioned to me was the accommodations that were put in place for a High Support Needs autistic boy who had been in one of her classes. She mentioned that having a visual schedule for his classes and activities for the day was really important to him, so he knew what to expect and could visually process each task that was coming up. This way, he wasn't being caught off guard or having to deal with unexpected changes because it had all been laid out for him ahead of time.

I've thought about this a lot and how, as autistic adults who were undiagnosed or unsupported throughout our childhood, our parents, carers and teachers never had these insights into how they could support us and ease our anxiety. Additionally, for those of us who were diagnosed later in life, even though we might have the same brains and the same needs as those who might have been diagnosed younger, we were never told any of these tips, tricks or strategies – which is why I set out to write this book in the first place. We might not have had parents or teachers making us visual schedules to help relax our nervous systems, but those things will still help to ease our anxiety at any stage of life, and so we can do them for ourselves.

A visual schedule could be a sequence of photographs, videos, line drawings, symbols, text, or other visual formats that are used to show the person using it what they are expected to do – such as the example on the opposite page. The series of visually presented tasks are arranged in the schedule in the order they are to be completed. This might look like:

- Sticking up photos of activities you're going to do that week, to prepare.

- Sticking up photos of friends you're seeing.

- Having symbols or drawings for each activity you need to do.

- Using a visual wall planner so you can see your schedule for the week.

I have a visual week planner that sticks to the wall and has a white-board coating so I can write on there and rub it off each week. Every Sunday, when I'm completing my **Big Brain Dump** (see **Tip 26, page 251**), I can fill out the big pre-arranged meetings or activities for the week on the planner. For me, words are enough – just being able to visually see ahead of time what I will be doing is enough to ease my anxiety, but you can also buy flashcards with drawings that show common activities on them if this would help you further.

Bonus tip: If you particularly struggle with a specific part of your schedule – like your morning or night-time routine – using the same idea of a visual schedule can be a helpful way to make sure you remember each task.

wake up · bathroom · take off pyjamas · put on clothes

eat · brush teeth · comb hair · bus

Tip 28:
Bare Minimum Monday

By Marisa-Jo Mayes (she/her), AuDHD founder of Space-Time Productivity

In the height of my (AuDHD) burnout, I used to begin each day with about ten things on my to-do list, but my functioning levels were so low that I would consistently complete only about two of them. Unless it had an immediate, strong consequence (like attending a meeting, replying to a client, or posting a contractual piece of content), my brain simply found it impossible. I'd yet to develop a self-compassionate lens through which to view myself, so I took this to mean any number of things about myself depending on the day: *I'm lazy, I'm bad at self-employment, I don't have the discipline it takes to be successful.*

This became a cycle. I used to stay up incredibly late every Sunday evening in an attempt to delay Monday as long as possible, knowing that a huge to-do list awaited me in the morning. On Monday, I'd sleep in until the last minute, the pressure to have a productive day (and therefore, week) rendering me completely frozen. The only thing that could force me into action was an approaching deadline, so I'd procrastinate everything until that point – which made the stress even worse.

After a few months of this, I woke up one Monday morning, looked at the list of ten things I thought Ideal Me should be able to accomplish, and in my gut, knew I would only do two of those things by the end of the day. I knew it. I thought to myself, *'What would happen if I just let this be acceptable?'* and I declared to my TikTok audience, 'This is your permission to do the absolute bare minimum today!' – **which was actually just permission I was extending to myself.**

On that first **Bare Minimum Monday**, I decided that instead of calling myself a horrible person for only being able to complete 20% of my to-do list, I would lower the bar and make that 20% my entire goal. I would only hold myself accountable to do the tasks that absolutely needed to be done that day, and anything I did beyond that would be icing on the cake. The weight of those eight other obligations having been lifted, I actually got the two done quickly. When my work was done, I went on a bike ride, cleaned my apartment, and even had enough momentum going to check off a couple more tasks. At the end of the day, I celebrated completing 200% of my goal (four tasks instead of two!) instead of internally berating myself for 'only completing four things'. This change felt so good that I knew I'd try it again the following week.

Six days later, the Sunday panic never set in. Instead, I felt relief. Since that day in early 2022, every single week has begun with a **Bare Minimum Monday** (and sometimes even bare minimum other days of the week!) – and I urge you to try it, too.

Tip 29:
Prioritizing for YOU

As I have mentioned earlier in this chapter, it is my belief that when people say that neurodivergent folks struggle with prioritization, they perhaps actually mean that we just don't prioritize the things that **they** think we should prioritize, in the way that **they** think we should prioritize them? Let me explain . . .

They might say that we're struggling to prioritize our careers . . .

When, in reality, we just don't want to make work our number one priority?

They might say that we're struggling to prioritize relationships . . .

When, in reality, we just don't put that specific relationship ahead of our own happiness and well-being?

They might say that we're struggling to prioritize the tasks that matter . . .

When, in reality, those tasks just don't matter as much to us?

Autistic people, especially, tend not to place as much importance on societal norms, expectations and hierarchies as neurotypical people do. As a result, they may be less likely to prioritize the things that society expects them to, or the things that other people consider of high importance. In our capitalist society, this might look like not prioritizing our career, as we explored earlier in the chapter, or not valuing finding a heteronormative, monogamous relationship as the 'most important' source of happiness.

Prioritization is all a matter of perspective, and so the **most important step** is prioritizing what is **most important to you**. Don't get me wrong; this can be a tricky thing to do in a society that expects us all to work in the same way, behave in the same way, want the same things and live the same lives. However, here are a few ways that you can get started:

- **Word of the month**
  As an alternative to setting New Year's resolutions at the start of January, you could choose a word or theme to prioritize at the beginning of each month. This word will then guide your decisions and behaviour throughout the month ahead. Some months, this might look like 'exercise' or 'health'; others, it could look like 'balance' or 'rest'; and others, it might look like 'connections' or 'relationships'. It's impossible to balance and prioritize every single thing all the time, so picking one priority for each month means that you can shift and change where your focus lies over time.

- **5 years – 1 year – 3 months – 1 month**
  A technique used for goal setting within ADHD coaching is working out your goals based on different things you'd like to achieve over a longer period of time. If you start by thinking of where you'd like to be, what you'd like to achieve, or what you'd like your life to look like in five years' time, you can then

start to strip this back and work out what you need to prioritize in the short term to get you to that end-point. For example, if, in five years' time, you'd like to be a *Sunday Times* bestselling author, in one year, you might want to have a book deal secured. To do this, you might want to have a book proposal finished in the next three months, and so over the next month, you need to prioritize researching 'how to structure a book proposal' and brain-dumping your key themes and points for the book. Splitting it down in this way can help you to know what to prioritize in the short term rather than procrastinating or getting overwhelmed by the big goal.

- **Working out your non-negotiables**
Spending the time to figure out what **you** need to feel your best means you know that you need to prioritize those things no matter what else might be going on in your life. For example, I know that reading and getting at least 10,000 steps per day are two things that are really important to keep me feeling good. Reading is one of the only things that keeps my brain fully zoned into one thing at a time, and going for a long walk both clears my head and makes sure that I'm tired enough to fall asleep at night. However, last year, when my first book, *unmasked*, was published and life got very busy, both of these things got pushed aside. I felt like I 'should' be prioritizing the work and that these were things that 'didn't matter too much' if they got pushed aside. In the end, that left me frazzled, burned

out and not feeling great. So now, I've made them non-negotiable things that I will prioritize **no matter what**. If that means I have to turn down a meeting because it's the only time I can get my steps in that day, then so be it. The world might tell me that I 'should' prioritize work, but actually, prioritizing getting out for a walk *is* prioritizing my career in the long run because it prevents me from getting burned out and needing to take time off.

Tip 30:
Start with the end

By Paff Evara (they/them), queer, neurodivergent Papuan Australian storyteller

Over the last year, I've curated an art show, created a magazine, hosted a two-day virtual conference and spun up a community in solidarity with Palestine — all while being a full-time creator. Each of these projects had a tonne of moving parts, and while hyper-focus can be a game-changer, organization and project management don't come naturally to my chaotic ADHD brain. This is why I use two guiding principles for every project: **find the why** and **start with the end**.

Find the why

'Why?' — a question that you might relate to a curious toddler, as their left-brain develops in a spurt, causing them to try and figure out how the world works. It's also a question that's always top of mind for me as a neurodivergent person: 'Why?' 'Why are we doing this?' 'Why are we doing it in this way?' often followed by questions like 'What are the objectives?' 'What does success look like?'

Clarifying questions are typically how I start any task, project or brief, as before I dive into anything, I want to know as much context as possible. This helps me to make sure whatever I put together is aligned with what they want to see. This is especially relevant when working with a client or a third party; by asking clarifying questions, I can typically mitigate miscommunications and misunderstandings, which are pretty commonplace when, as an autistic person, you might miss the underlying social cues and assumptions.

After I've gathered as much context as possible, I move on to the second principle:

Start with the end

Rather than thinking of what tasks I need to complete next, I like to project myself forward to the **very end** of the project. I know the why, and this process helps me visualize exactly what that end product/experience/deliverable needs to look like. Using that final goal and deadline, I can then work backwards and map out the milestones I need to hit to reach that.

Using a magazine launch as an example, to hit the final deadline I need to have a printed magazine, a website ready for launch, and marketing content. For me to have the marketing collateral, I need to have the printed magazine – so that has to be created first. I also know there is a two-week printing turnaround for the magazine, so I need to allow for that time-frame in my plans, too. I keep working backwards until I get to the start, which helps me to ensure no essential tasks are missing along the way. Naturally, you might enjoy plugging this into a project management board (ideally something visual) to stay organized, plus get that sweet, sweet dopamine for each task completed.

With any project, there will, of course, be stumbling blocks, hurdles or additional tasks that pop up that you hadn't foreseen. But by **starting with the end**, you always have an eye on your final vision, goal and objective, which can help you prioritize and focus – two things that are essential for neurodivergent brains that are easily distracted.

Planning and prioritization recap

Planning and prioritization is the executive functioning skill that gives us the ability to create a systematic approach to achieving goals, including breaking tasks into steps and determining their relative importance. It's what allows us to take a big end goal, and work backwards to figure out what we need to do to get there; the map that gives us the route we need to get to the finish line. The way that neurodivergent brains work means that we are often taking in and processing a much greater amount of information, which means there are a lot more things to sift through, making prioritization more difficult for us. Additionally, we are often missing the context that neurotypical people naturally glean, so we may need to ask more clarifying questions in order to gather all the information we need to be able to know how to plan, prioritize and move forward.

In this chapter, we have explored:

- What planning and prioritization is.

- The systems which have affected the way we think about planning and prioritization.

- Some ways we can support ourselves with planning and prioritization.

- 5 things to consider putting in place for your planning and prioritization.

Your takeaway box

- Autistic people generally process information in a bottom-up way, which is the opposite of how most neurotypical or allistic people process. This means that we are constantly taking in a lot of sensory input in order to build the picture of what's around us. Not only is this tiring, but it also means that there is a lot more information that we need to sift through in order to prioritize compared to neurotypical people, and we might need to ask more clarifying questions.

- Often, when people suggest that others are 'bad at prioritizing', they might instead mean that that person hasn't prioritized the things that they think they should, in the way that they think they should prioritize them. We are all individual and unique human beings, which means that we will all value and prioritize different things, and that is okay!

- Planning and prioritization are all based on context. The circumstances and context of a situation are what determine which pieces of information or tasks are the most important to do, so creating that context for yourself (with rules like your word of the month or your non-negotiables) or asking other people for clarification of that context can be good ways to help you move forward.

7

Task initiation

Have you ever had that feeling where you know what you need to get going with, and you actually really **do** want to get going with it, but no matter how hard you try, you just can't get your brain to play ball? Instead, you're stuck, maybe scrolling on your phone or lying in bed, with the voice inside your head yelling at you to JUST GET UP AND DO THE THING, but physically unable to get started? If you're an ADHDer like me, then the chances are that this is a very common occurrence – for me, I'd say it happens multiple times a day, at least.

Task initiation (or our struggles with it) is what puts us in this position; as neurodivergent people (ADHDers especially), we often have **interest-led brains**, which means that, with all the 'willpower' in the world, unless we have the perfect combination of external motivation to get us going, we just cannot get started with the things that we need to. But, do not fear, although task initiation might be one of the executive functions that disables us the most, it is actually one of the easiest to work around, or 'hack'. When we learn what it is exactly that motivates our interest-led brains, we can incorporate these things into the tasks that we need to do in order to make getting going a whole lot easier.

In this chapter, we will explore:

- What is task initiation?

- Which systems have affected the way we think about task initiation?

- How can we support ourselves with task initiation?

- 5 things to consider putting in place for your task initiation

When it comes
to ADHDers,
simply knowing
that something
is important isn't
enough; our interest-
led brains need
another motivating
factor to get started.

We need to take away the presumption that if we cannot immediately start any task on demand without hesitation or procrastination then something is 'wrong', and instead see that hesitation and procrastination are necessary parts of the process.

What is task initiation?

Our next executive functioning skill, **task initiation**, is defined as the ability to independently begin a task or activity without procrastination or hesitation. It is the green light, the gas pedal, which moves us from simply **thinking** about doing something to **actually getting on with it**. This skill is particularly tricky for neurodivergent folks, especially ADHDers, because, as mentioned in the introduction to this chapter, we often have **interest-led**, rather than **importance-led** or **priority-led**, brains.

To explain what I mean by interest-led brains it's perhaps helpful to start by explaining how people who don't have ADHD are able to motivate themselves to get started with a task. They are generally able to motivate themselves to do something simply because they know it is important, either to them personally or to the people around them. Even if they aren't interested in it or don't enjoy it, this **importance** is enough reason for their brains to get going. For example, they might not enjoy doing laundry, but they know that it is important that it gets done, and knowing this is enough motivation to get started.

However, when it comes to ADHDers, simply knowing that something is important isn't enough; our interest-led brains need another motivating factor to get started. It is believed this is because ADHD brains regulate dopamine, the neurotransmitter responsible for stimulating us, in a different way than non-ADHD brains. Dopamine is known as the 'reward' hormone and plays an important role in memory, movement, motivation, mood, attention and more.

Research has shown that people with ADHD have at least one defective gene, the DRD2 gene, which makes it difficult for neurons to respond to dopamine. The research in this area is very limited, but it has been suggested that where most people (non-ADHDers) have a fairly regular stream of dopamine (they do a task, they get rewarded, and that reward keeps them motivated), ADHD brains generally have a lower level of dopamine (which means we will struggle to concentrate or get started with things), and then when we do become interested in something, we will have a flood of too much dopamine (which might cause our intense hyperfocus states). This is one of the reasons that the name Attention Deficit Hyperactivity Disorder is considered to be inaccurate; it is not that we have a **deficit** of attention, it's that our brains don't **regulate** dopamine levels in the same way as people who don't have ADHD.

Although this is all a huge simplification of our brain's complicated chemistry, thinking about my ADHD in regards to its dopamine levels has really helped me to work out how to get started on tasks by supporting myself to make task initiation easier. As a very logical problem solver, I started to think of it as an equation: if my brain generally has less dopamine than it needs to complete a task, and the task itself isn't providing me with enough dopamine to get and stay motivated, all I need to do is top up the task with a little extra dopamine hit which will allow me to hit that magic threshold of motivation to get started. We'll explore what sort of things we can add to tasks for that extra dopamine hit later in the chapter, but hopefully, this novel way of thinking about task initiation will help you in the same way that it helped me.

Which systems have affected the way we think about task initiation?

When reading Sonny Jane Wise's book **We're All Neurodiverse**, I was struck by their explanation of executive functioning not as skills, but instead as a list of **rules** that society has imposed on us. They included a quote from Jesse Meadows (they/them), a writer and digital artist whose Medium blog focuses on critical ADHD studies and re-politicizing mental health, who explains:

> Most people on social media seem to think the set of skills around planning, organizing, focusing, and time management which we call 'executive function' is a structure in the brain, not a concept made up by a bunch of white male doctors who idolize business men so much they modeled an entire neurological value system off of them.

This is essentially a much more direct way of explaining the concept that we have explored throughout the book: the idea that a lot of the ways in which we are expected to function are simply a list of 'shoulds' imposed on us by our society and the systems of oppression within it. However, Sonny's explanation of the expectations around task initiation, in particular, really got me thinking. They explained that the way we currently expect people's task initiation to work is essentially society saying, 'You must be able to start any task immediately on demand whether or not it's something you actually want to do or are interested in.'

When we put it this way, we can see that, in reality, this is a ludicrous expectation. It doesn't take into account people's preferences, interests or circumstances. One community which is particularly affected by these unrealistic expectations is the disabled and chronically ill community. They might not have the energy, capacity or ability to immediately start any task on demand, and also may need to consider the consequences of doing that task that they will be faced with later, such as a crash or flare-up. As Lozza Gilbert (they/them), multiply disabled activist, creator and writer, explains:

> With task initiation, there are so many factors that you have to weigh up and kind of calculate before you start doing a task. For me, because there's the mix of autism, ADHD and chronic illness, I find that if one thing is going 'right', something else will inevitably be going 'wrong'. So even if I have the energy to start the task in terms of not feeling fatigued, my ADHD is going to be cropping up like, 'Yeah, well, you don't have the executive functioning to do this.' So either way, there's always something that stops me from initiating a task. It's very hard to kind of just be like, 'Yes, this task that needs doing, I will start doing it.'

> As an example, when writing an article, I have to think about, 'Okay, well, I won't be in bed, I might be sat at my desk, so I'll be more upright

for a longer period of time.' And being upright is expending energy. I've then got to try and concentrate for an extended period of time, which is also energy draining – especially when you've got multiple different disabilities that mean that concentrating is ridiculously hard. And then you've got to think about the actual physical effort doing research or reading, or actually processing words on a page, and things like that. There are so many factors of each task that you have to weigh up, so you have to think, 'Do I have the physical capacity to start it? If I start the task, is this gonna then mess up my health for the next however many days or weeks?' So you end up meticulously planning your days, just so that you can account for how much energy you have, and how much energy you might have afterwards. You have to think ahead a lot.

Additionally, something that I find really interesting with regard to task initiation is how we think about time. I first came across Marta Rose's (also known as @divergent_design_studios) concept of **neuroemergent time** in a writing course that I did with KR Moorhead (who you'll hear from in **Tip 31: Replacing demands with permissions, page 288**), and it made a lot of sense in explaining the ways that I experience time as an autistic ADHDer.

Marta Rose explains that the way we currently measure time (under late capitalism and White supremacy culture) is not objectively the

only or 'correct' way of measuring time; it is simply a construct which they call 'industrial time'. The way that we currently measure in hours, days and weeks was constructed around a factory model of work that served to function employers who managed vast numbers of employees who were expected to achieve set tasks in set amounts of time, rather than being a real, natural or accurate way of measuring time. In the words of Marta, 'This is time as it has been imposed on us by industrial capitalism, fueled by white supremacy.' After dismantling industrial time as a concept, they go on to explore other ways that we can explore time which might feel more authentic to our natural rhythms and experiences as neurodivergent people, such as seeing time in more seasonal or cyclical ways, and offer two main theories:

1. Spiral time

When we see time as spiral rather than linear, we remove the idea that 'progress' comes from us moving forward in a straight line towards some fixed point or end goal. Instead, our progress is just the act of moving around the spiral, and our goals are things that emerge along the way. By seeing time as a spiral, we can also 'zoom out' from the time-frames in which we are measuring goals or success. For example, under linear or industrial time, if you start a degree course and do not complete it in the assigned three-year time-frame, this would be seen as a failure. However, under spiral time, you can see the learnings that you took from the parts of the course that you did complete as a success, and know that you'll come back to and use these learnings later on in time as your spiral brings you back around to them. Marta encourages us to think of past experiences or 'uncompleted' projects as 'buried treasure' that will be available for us to dig back up later in the spiral.

2. Elliptical time

The second paradigm for time that Marta offers is elliptical time, shown in the diagram below, which encourages us to think of time as an elliptical orbit – where some parts of the orbit are really fast and productive (around the tight bends), while other parts of the orbit are much slower (in what they call 'spinning out in space gathering stardust'). Both parts of the orbit are necessary to complete the ellipse, and even when you feel as though you're stuck in the slow, spinning-out-in-space phase (which you might have previously been told was 'executive dysfunction'), you're always on your way back to another fast, tight bend.

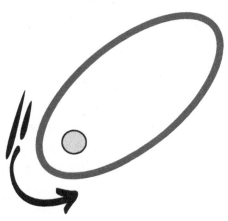

Elliptical time, especially, feels very accurate for me as an ADHDer who jumps from periods of intense, hyperproductive focus where I will achieve more than seems humanly possible, to periods of lull and slow where even doing the simplest of tasks feels impossible. Take writing this book, for example:

- When my editor, Amy, first mentioned the idea of the book to me, I was excited, motivated and focused. This was a fast phase, where lots of ideas were coming together all at once while I was in the tight bend of the ellipse.

- Then, when I went through the period of struggling to know how to pull it all together properly, as I explained in the introduction, I was in a period of spinning out in space, needing the time around the orbit for my brain to connect the dots and bring things together.

- Next, we came back around to the tight bend, where my concept all clicked together in my mind, and I found my hyperfocus, writing out my first few chapters in the space of a couple of weeks.

- Then, inevitably, once this tight bend had passed, I went spinning back into space. Once I had hyperfocused my way through the first few chapters, there was a long period where I just could not motivate myself to sit down and get writing. I felt as though I could feel all the ideas and parts moving around in my brain, but, no matter how hard I tried, I just could not make any real 'progress' in terms of words on a page and really started to beat myself up that I wasn't going to get it done before my deadline.

- However, now that my deadline is quickly approaching and the urgency has kicked in (more on this in the next section), I'm back to firing on all cylinders and working through chapters at a rapid pace. I've whizzed through around 20,000 words in the last couple of weeks, and it's all coming together much more quickly than I could have imagined even three weeks ago when I felt stuck, spinning out in space.

When thinking of time as linear, or through the lens of what Marta calls industrial time, it is very easy during periods of low motivation to be hard on myself. During the time after my initial hyperfocus had passed I fell into the trap of thinking things like 'The weeks are flying by and you're nowhere near where you should be by this point. Over three-quarters of the time has passed, and you're not even halfway through your word count!' I could say that I have 'executive dysfunction', and blame myself for procrastinating, not trying hard enough, being lazy or just generally a rubbish person.

However, if I instead view my writing experience through the paradigm of elliptical time, I can see that each phase is a necessary and inevitable part of the process. The hyperfocused, über-productive phases will come, and, inevitably, they will also pass. The periods of 'spinning out in space' aren't a failure, laziness, or anything to panic about; they are just part of the cycle and, in their own way, are preparing me to be able to get back to the fast phases. It's a time to slow down, process, think of the bigger picture, and even rest, so that my brain and body are ready and raring to go through the tight bends. If we use this way of thinking to change our views on task initiation, we can take away the presumption that if we cannot immediately start any task on demand without hesitation or procrastination then something is 'wrong', and instead see that hesitation and procrastination are necessary parts of the process in our ellipse of time.

Marta Rose's description of industrial time is further backed up by some of Tema Okun's characteristics of White supremacy culture. The first of these characteristics is **urgency**, which refers to our cultural habit of applying a sense of urgency to our everyday lives. We are constantly in a rush, and everything has to be done on demand, immediately, and completed in a short amount of time. We value speed, quick decision-making, and immediate action, often at the expense of thoroughness, reflection, or consideration of different perspectives.

This sense of urgency shows little regard for the actual amount of time something requires, disconnects us from our need to breathe, pause and reflect, and means that we're so busy jumping from urgent task to urgent task that we never have the time to consider the bigger picture or deal with ongoing systemic issues such as White supremacy and other systems of oppression.

How urgency affects the way we see task initiation and executive functioning:

- We are told that we must be able to do anything that is required of us immediately and on demand, which informs the way we define what is considered 'normal' vs 'disordered' task initiation.

- A culture of urgency prioritizes quick results and doesn't consider the energy used (or difficulties faced) in effectively planning, organizing and executing tasks. This puts a huge pressure on us to be not only always using our executive functioning skills, but also using them at a rapid pace.

- An emphasis on speed and urgency means that anyone who needs more time to process information or complete tasks is considered lesser or incompetent when this is not the case.

Additionally, White supremacy culture also causes us to value **quantity over quality**.

Quantity over quality defines the belief that the things which we can count, track and measure are the most important. As an example, we might value having a higher number of followers on social media rather than having a smaller, more meaningful community, or having a bigger, more profitable business rather than a smaller one that is doing more meaningful work. It explains the way we might feel it is 'better' to get through as many individual tasks on our to-do list as possible than it would be to do fewer tasks, but do them well. Quantity over quality values speed, urgency, money and 'growth' over the process, meaning, and importance behind the work that we do.

How quantity over quality affects the way we see task initiation and executive functioning:

- An emphasis on quantity often prioritizes the sheer volume of output or tasks completed over the quality of execution or the process involved. This causes us to disregard the energy required for things like organizing, planning, task initiation or flexibility, which can be much more tricky for neurodivergent folks.

- The common expectation is for us to complete various different tasks throughout the day, which means we have to begin each of these tasks individually, putting a huge strain on our task initiation. If, instead, we were to focus on one longer, more meaningful task, or have the capacity to work on one project fully at a time, we would have less to initiate and then be able to finish it to completion efficiently, rather than struggling to initiate a hundred different tasks throughout the day.

- We are expected to constantly be churning out more and more work, which means that our sole purpose might be seen as 'to produce' or 'to work', which determines which skills are deemed more desirable or important than others, i.e. our ability to start tasks quickly is deemed to be more important than our ability to finish those tasks at the highest quality.

How can we support ourselves with task initiation?

As mentioned earlier in the chapter, when it comes to task initiation it can be helpful to think of our ADHD as an equation. If our brains generally have less dopamine than they need to complete a task, and the task itself doesn't provide us with enough dopamine to get and stay motivated, all we need to do is top up the task with a little extra dopamine hit to reach the threshold. As I said earlier, this is a **very** simplified account of what is actually going on in our very complicated and complex brains, and much more research is needed to work out the reality of the hormones and neurotransmitters that affect the way we function. However, it can be a simple framework in helping us to find ways of best supporting ourselves and learning to work **with** our brains rather than against them.

So if we're considering it to be a case of finding little dopamine top-ups that we can add to tasks to make them more appealing, it is helpful to know what it actually **is** that motivates our interest-led brains. The four things that best motivate ADHDers are usually defined as:

1. Interest

The first thing that motivates our interest-led brains is, of course, something that we find interesting, such as a topic we're enthusiastic about or something that makes us curious. It makes sense that if something is interesting to us, we're naturally going to be motivated to get started with it – but how can we use this to motivate ourselves to do something we're *not* interested in? Well, in these cases, we can either find the interesting parts of a project we're working on and start there, or we can find ways of weaving other things that we're interested in into the task that doesn't feel as interesting.

For example, if you know that you're a lover of spreadsheets, you could create a spreadsheet to plan out the task you need to do, or if you're really into films, you could find a film about the topic you need to study.

2. Novelty

Our next motivator is something that is novel, or new. This can apply to tasks that we've never done before or tasks that feel as though they are leading us on a new, exciting adventure. This explains why ADHDers tend to have a love of learning new things, because the novelty factor motivates our brains and keeps us interested. We can use novelty to make other less exciting tasks more appealing to our interest-led brains by regularly changing the types of tasks we're working on, trying to solve old problems in new ways, or adding something new while we're doing a not-new task.

This could look like working from a café that you've never been to before instead of working from home every day, or buying yourself a new notepad or stationery for your study project.

3. Challenge

Our third motivator is something that is challenging to us or something that involves an element of competition.

This competition could be against ourselves, such as seeing how many words we're able to write in a

thirty-minute period and trying to break our record
each day, or against other people, such as having
an accountability partner or joining leaderboards on
apps like Duolingo that encourage you to learn a new
language.

4. Urgency

Our final motivator is when something is urgent,
and has a tight, time-based deadline, which is why
many of us might find that we can only get things
done at the very last minute (I'm looking at myself
typing out these words when my book deadline is a
measly four days away [which might make you think,
'Wow, Ellie, that's quite tight, but at least you're
not writing it the night before!', but, really, I go on
holiday tomorrow and I want to get it finished before
I go so . . . I told you I'm far from having it all figured
out myself!!!]).

This could look like inviting a friend round so
you're forced to tidy up before they come, or asking
your manager to set you lots of shorter deadlines
to complete different parts of a project rather than
having one long deadline and knowing that you'll
leave it all until the last minute.

Most of the tips that you'll find throughout the rest of the chapter
involve adding either interest, novelty, challenge or urgency to a
task in some way to help motivate you to get started, but, once you
know that these are the main things that appeal to our interest-led

brains, you can find different ways to add them to basically any task that you need to get done!

A list of things that are <u>absolutely fine</u>:

- Not being able to immediately start any task on demand without prior warning.

- Needing to pair tasks together to make them more stimulating, for example listening to music while working, or watching your favourite TV show while exercising.

- Starting with the easier, more appealing tasks first to build up to the bigger, more important tasks.

- Relying on accountability or rewards to get things done.

- Leaving things until the last minute if you know that urgency is the only motivator that works for you.

- Doing seemingly unrelated tasks before the main task that you need to do, not to procrastinate but because you need a clear workspace before you sit down to write, for example.

- Doing fewer tasks each day, rather than thinking that you need to be in 'go' mode every second of every day.

- Taking the time to decompress or scroll on your phone between tasks without beating yourself up for putting other things off.

- Getting started with two minutes of a task rather than thinking you have to commit to sitting down for multiple hours so that it's easier to come back to when you're ready.

- Working outside the traditional '9 to 5' working hours if you know that you're more productive in the early mornings or the evenings.

Tip 31:
Replacing demands with permissions

By KR Moorhead (they/them), AuDHD writer, mentor and facilitator, and creator of A Crash Course in Writing While Neurodivergent

When recently asked to write about what feelings I associate with 'beginnings', I found that words like **frustrated**, **tired**, **anxious** and **bored** came to mind, specifically when considering tasks with foreseeable endings, like writing projects, event planning or launching new courses.

My tendency towards perfectionism and an all-or-nothing mentality mean I struggle to really define what counts as 'work'. Have you heard the saying, 'If you can't do something right, don't do it at all'? I certainly have, and I feel like many neurodivergent people have taken this advice to heart. If we aren't doing the exact task we think we should be doing, exactly the way we think we should be doing it, then we feel like we are wasting our time.

When we tell ourselves, 'I should be doing such-and-such right now', or 'I should be doing it this particular way', we are essentially creating a demand, which can cause us to shut down to the task altogether, even if it is something we really want to do.

One way we can attempt to break down the barriers to task initiation is to turn our **'shoulds' into things we are allowed to do** – replacing **demands** with **permissions**.

First, it can be helpful to make a list of the **'shoulds'** we attach to our working practice. For a writer, this may look something like this:

I feel like I should . . .

- **Write every day.**

- **Write in the mornings.**

- **Write 'worthwhile' content.**

- **Write 'sellable' content.**

- **Write the whole time I am working.**

- **Write as much as or more than I did yesterday.**

Try to unpick each of these. Where did this expectation actually come from? Why do you feel you should do this? Are you ascribing moral value to things that do not have moral value? (i.e. if we can't write every day, we are somehow 'bad').

Then, write a list of permissions you give yourself instead. Things you are allowed to do during your working time that may not be the work itself but are tangential to it. Again, for a writer, this may look like . . .

I am allowed to . . .

- **Daydream.**

- **Read a book.**

- **Listen to music.**

- **Talk to a friend about writing.**

- **Work on any project that interests me right now.**

- **Tidy my workspace.**

What this achieves is twofold. First, these things are often a necessary part of our work that we don't usually recognize as work. Sometimes, we feel these are things that are keeping us from our work, when really they are integral to it. Second, by recognizing these activities as 'work', we allow ourselves multiple small opportunities to succeed, instead of fail. If we tell ourselves that we are meant to be actively 'working' the whole time we are in our workspace, then we might see daydreaming as a failure. Once we include daydreaming in our working practice, when we find ourselves doing it – we have actually succeeded and can benefit from the motivation this gives us.

Below you will find a space to write your own list of 'coulds'. Once you've made your list, post it in a prominent position and keep adding to it as you discover more and more activities that are part of your practice. Next time you are struggling to initiate a task, you can trick your brain into getting past the block by starting with something on this list. This success will give your brain a boost of energy, making it more willing to continue.

I am allowed to . . .

- _____

- _____

- _____

- _____

- _____

Tip 32:
Morning routine playlist

As we explored earlier in the chapter, adding novelty, urgency, challenge and interest to a task is the best way to get our interest-led brains to play ball with the things we want them to do. One of my favourite ways to do this is to implement a **morning routine playlist**.

For me, sticking to a quick and simple morning routine is the best chance I have of actually getting out of the house or on with the tasks that I need to without getting distracted. If I give myself the time and space to do a long skincare routine, make a complicated breakfast, take a shower, style my hair and do my make-up, it is pretty much dead certain that I'll get lost in one of these tasks or just end up taking **way** too much time. So, instead, I like to keep things short and simple:

- Hair slicked back.

- Eyebrow gel on and tinted moisturizer on.

- Toaster waffles and a protein shake or protein yoghurt for breakfast.

- Medication taken.

- Clothes on.

- Teeth brushed.

- DONE!

However, no matter how simple this routine is, my brain is still likely to a) refuse to get started and instead want to lie in bed scrolling on my phone all morning, or b) end up taking way too long on each task and/or get distracted (my brain will *always* find something to get distracted by). So, to keep myself on track, I've created a playlist on Spotify, where **one song is assigned to each task**. So I'll have one song to which I will get out of bed, one song during which I do my hair, one song during which I do my brows and moisturizer, and so on, and so on.

This adds **urgency** and **challenge** to the morning because I only have a limited amount of time to complete each task, and it adds novelty since I'm starting the day by listening to some of my favourite songs. (You might want to switch up your playlist every week or so if you're somebody who gets bored with listening to the same songs over and over again, but this autistic gal could happily listen to the same 2006 indie bangers every day for the rest of her life.)

If you're someone who needs to get up and out to prevent getting distracted, a morning routine playlist could be a great addition to your day, or you can also use this technique to add challenge, urgency and novelty to other parts of your day:

- **You could see how much tidying away you can get done before your favourite song finishes.**

- **You could challenge yourself to put the food shop away before the end of the playlist.**

- **You could see how many words you can write during the length of your favourite album.**

- You could give yourself a one-song-scrolling-break to put a time limit on your phone-checking between tasks.

Below, you can find space to list out your morning routine tasks and choose a song you might like to play for each.

Bonus tip: To add more novelty and remind yourself of the task you're supposed to be doing, you could find songs that have lyrics or titles that relate to each task. For example, I like to use 'T-Shirt Weather' by Circa Waves as my getting-dressed song, and 'I've Just Seen a Face' by the Beatles for my skincare/make-up song!

- _____

_____

_____

- _____

_____

_____

- _____

_____

_____

- _____

_____

_____

Tip 33:
Body-doubling

Do you ever find that you can get started with tasks and do things so much more easily when you're surrounded by people doing the same? Whether that's working in an office instead of at home by yourself, or cooking when someone else is in the kitchen, it could be thanks to something known as **body-doubling**.

Body-doubling is kind of what it says on the tin – you work on the task that you need to, while another person (your **body-double**) works alongside you. It's a really quick and easy way to add accountability to a task since you're more likely to get on with the task (rather than avoiding it by scrolling on your phone, for example) when you know somebody is watching you. It also takes advantage of our natural inclination to mask by mimicking the people around us. Although masking can be tiresome in many circumstances, if our natural reaction is to copy the person next to us who is getting on with their work, then we can use this to our advantage!

There are a few ways that you can use body-doubling to help you get on with the tasks you need to:

- If you work from home by yourself, working from a café or co-working space where other people are also working can help to keep you accountable.

- You could also virtually body-double via Zoom or Google Meet and keep the video stream of your friend working alongside you on your screen while you work. There are even online communities and platforms where you can join group body-doubling sessions or find body-doubles to work with.

- You could ask a friend to come round to your house while you clean, as just having someone there will help you to get started, even if they're not doing much to help.

- You could ask your partner, parent or housemate to join you in the kitchen while you cook.

I have a weekly recurring meeting in my calendar for a body-doubling session with my friend Charli (who you're actually going to hear from in the next tip!) every Monday morning, so we can both start our week with a productive hour of individually ticking off some of our to-dos while having the other person there to keep us accountable. We've also frequently toyed with hosting virtual body-doubling sessions for the (un)masked community (the online and IRL community for neurodivergent people that I founded in 2022), so please drop us a message on Instagram @weareunmasked if this is something you'd like to join.

Tip 34:
Slower start morning routines

By Charli Clement (they/she), author of All Tangled Up in Autism and Chronic Illness *and autism and psychiatric care lived experience practitioner, speaker, creator and writer*

As an autistic ADHDer with chronic illness, my morning routine is critical to the type of day that I have. My fatigue, pain and sensory needs don't disappear just because I've had a good morning routine, don't get me wrong — but starting slower and with more intention means my body is slightly more relaxed, and my brain feels less frantic.

Before introducing a slower, more targeted morning routine, I was constantly waking up over-stimulated and often trying to get ready for the day in ten minutes to get every single second of sleep I could to try and reduce fatigue. Now, I get slightly less sleep, but I am in a better position. I wake up over a longer period and don't immediately push myself into action, and it's also easier to make the transition between tasks because there is longer to do so. Maybe part of the reason we struggle to get started with tasks is that our brains and bodies haven't been given the opportunity to get ready, or to warm up to the expectations placed on them.

Some of the things that my slower start morning routine includes are:

- **Sunrise alarm clock**
  Using one of these means that I start to wake up subconsciously with the light before I wake properly,

over the space of half an hour. Sometimes, I wake up halfway through; sometimes, I don't wake up until the audio prompt – but it means I wake up at the right moment rather than suddenly. The lack of a loud audio alarm being the first sensory input also stops me from immediately pushing into over-stimulation (which exacerbates my pain and fatigue).

- **Reading before picking up my phone**
I used to always go on social media the second I woke up and then get stuck in bed doomscrolling. Now, I use my e-reader for a minimum of five minutes before I'm allowed to go on my phone to break that cycle. I've found it means I get less stuck on my phone throughout the rest of the day, too, because I haven't immediately given my brain a mega-dose of stimulation that it will then be trying to match for the rest of the day.

- **Brain-dump and check calendar**
The second I wake up, my brain is going – the internal hyperactivity kicks in and I'll immediately be having six different trains of thought. I brain-dump all my thoughts down and then make sure I know what's happening during the day so I don't feel uncertain about the day's structure.

- **Breakfast**
I make sure I fuel my body in the morning, even if I'm not ready to eat super early in the day. Protein is great for ADHDers (such as eggs or a protein yoghurt!), but just making sure I eat **something** is the main thing.

- **Habit-stacking**

  I habit-stack taking my medication, doing my skincare and brushing my teeth. I do these tasks together, one after the other, at the same time and in the same place each day to make sure they happen. You could habit-stack any of your morning routine tasks if one of them often gets forgotten or feels harder to complete. Sometimes, I use visual timers to stop myself from losing track of time, too.

Making your morning routine work for you is the main thing — it doesn't need to have twenty steps or be perfect every single day like you see in people's aesthetic Instagram videos! You might want to add other things — perhaps some movement, stretches, or a workout in the morning might help you focus, or preparing lunch for work means you won't impulse spend. I think it's a process of trial and error. I'm still adjusting mine now, and I don't always manage to get it all done. Don't beat yourself up — it's more about slowing down and taking stock of what supports the rest of your day.

Tip 35:
Quick tick treat

While neurotypical people might find long-term rewards and treats enough motivation to get going with a task, our interest-led ADHD brains often need something a bit more immediate. Our brains tend to see time as 'now' or 'not now', so knowing that we'll get a reward at the end of a task, or that we'll feel better in the future for getting it done, feels a bit too abstract to get us motivated. For example, knowing that we'll feel healthier and happier after six weeks of exercising isn't going to be enough to get us off the sofa right this second to go for a run. We're not too concerned with what **future** us will get out of it; we need to know what **current** us will get out of it **right here, right now**.

To use this to our advantage, we can implement **immediate rewards for getting started** with a task, rather than thinking we have to finish something completely to earn the treat. This could look like:

- If you love a morning coffee, you can have it as a treat while you work, but **only** once you've got started with your emails.

- If you have a certain favourite comfort show, you could treat yourself to having it on in the background, but **only** while you're getting work done.

- You could enjoy some snacks while tidying your room, but **only** once you've started.

These little rewards trigger the pleasure centre in the brain to release dopamine, which helps the brain associate doing the task with feeling good.

Below, you can make a list of some of the tasks you regularly need to get done and some treats that you could pair each task with to help you get started.

What I need to get done	Treat I could have for getting started

Task initiation recap

Task initiation is, very simply, the process of getting started. It is defined as the ability to independently begin a task or activity without procrastination or hesitation; however, as we've explored throughout the chapter, perhaps these expectations are far too high. Human beings have always been social creatures, so maybe it's okay if we can't get started with things completely independently and need a little encouragement or a push in the right direction from the people around us. And maybe, time isn't as linear as we've previously been told, and what looks from the outside to be 'procrastination' or 'hesitation' is actually just us taking the time that we need to prepare, rest, process, think, reflect, gather our thoughts, plan, or do other things.

In this chapter, we have explored:

- What task initiation is.

- The systems which have affected the way we think about task initiation.

- Some ways we can support ourselves with task initiation.

- 5 things to consider putting in place for your task initiation.

Your takeaway box

- ADHD brains, especially, are interest-led. This means that our brains aren't motivated to do something simply because we know that it is important, or we know that we 'should'. Instead, we need to add a little extra stimulation in the form of **interest** (adding something we're interested in to a project that otherwise doesn't interest us), **novelty** (doing new things, or adding something new and exciting to a task), **challenge** (making something into a competition, either against ourselves or other people), or **urgency** (adding a tight, time-based deadline).

- We have been led to believe, because of capitalism and White supremacy, that time moves in a straight line, but this isn't the only way that we can think of time. For neurodivergent people, it might be helpful to think of time in terms of seasons, spirals or elliptical orbits, as these better explain our experiences and ways of being and doing.

- Sometimes, not being able to start a task can be disabling, but sometimes it is just our body or brain's way of letting us know that we need time to rest, time to process, or time to think. Being able to start any task on demand with no support, without taking into account our needs, preferences or circumstances, is an unrealistic expectation that we can learn to let go of.

8

Organization

Like with planning, I feel as though I go from one extreme to another in terms of organization. The autistic side of my brain loves nothing more than counting things out, colour-coding and labelling, re-organizing my wardrobe, and spending hours (or even days) creating a complicated notion board that 'is *definitely* going to be the answer to getting my shit together once and for all!' Unfortunately, however, there is another side of me that couldn't be more different: my ADHD. This side of me is messy, disorganized, usually running late and trying to juggle a million things all at once in something that resembles somewhat of a hurricane or tornado.

I think organization, out of all the executive functions, is something that we as a society have assigned a huge amount of moral value to. Being organized makes you a Good Person; someone who is thoughtful, professional, 'grown-up' and going to go far in life. If organization is something that doesn't come naturally to you, though, often these struggles or differences will very quickly be labelled as personal flaws: you're lazy, you're selfish, you're care-less and you can't be trusted. There is nothing 'careless' about a neurodivergent person's struggles with organization, though; in fact, we often care greatly about the things that we do. It's simply that our brains aren't designed to do things in the way that our neuronormative, capitalist society expects us to.

In this chapter, we will explore:

- What is organization?

- Which systems have affected the way we think about organization?

- How can we support ourselves with organization?

- 5 things to consider putting in place for your task organization.

As long as things feel organized, or helpful, to <u>you</u>, then it doesn't matter what they look like to anybody else.

There are no prizes for doing life in hard mode, and by letting go of some of the 'sounds' we've had imposed on us, we can make life a whole lot easier for ourselves.

What is organization?

Our final executive functioning skill, organization, is defined as the ability to structure and arrange information, materials or physical spaces. This could be organizing the things in our homes to be stored away tidily, it could be keeping our schedules organized in order to make sure we're always where we need to be when we need to be there, or it could be organizing files on our computers so that we're able to find them when we need them. Organization is something that everybody struggles with from time to time, with research suggesting that the average person loses up to **nine** items every day – or 198,743 in a lifetime – with phones, keys, sunglasses and paperwork topping the list. However, neurodivergent folks might have an especially hard time staying organized for a variety of reasons, which we can explore by working through the diagnostic criteria for ADHD outlined in the DSM-5, and figuring out what is really going on:

- **Often fails to give close attention to details or makes careless mistakes in schoolwork, at work, or with other activities.**
  The ability to pay attention to and keep track of small details is essential when staying organized, whereas ADHDers (and other neurodivergent people) generally tend to think in more of a big-picture way.

- **Often has trouble organizing tasks and activities.**
  We can struggle to organize tasks and activities, which could also be linked to our struggles with planning and

prioritization (more on this in **Chapter 6: Planning and prioritization, page 236**) and working memory (more on this in **Chapter 1: Working memory, page 57**). Tasks, projects and activities generally have lots of different moving parts, which can be tricky for our brains to keep track of all at once, or prioritize in order of importance.

- **Often loses things necessary for tasks and activities (e.g. school materials, pencils, books, tools, wallets, keys, paperwork, eyeglasses, mobile telephones).**
  A big part of organization is thinking ahead to what we will need to get something done (for example, remembering that we need to take our gym kit to work with us so we can go to the gym after work), and storing those things in a way that means we're able to find them when we need them. As we explored in **Tip 3: Showroom chic (page 81)**, ADHDers can have differences in what is known as object constancy or object permanence. This means that we experience 'out of sight, out of mind' – so if something isn't in our direct line of sight, we forget it exists. This makes it very hard to keep track of where all of our things are at any given time, making it difficult to stay organized.

- **Is often easily distracted.**
  As we discovered in **Chapter 7: Task initiation (page 267)**, ADHD brains (and those of other neurodivergent people) are often interest-led, meaning that we aren't motivated to do things just because we know that we 'should' or because we know that they

are important in the same ways as neurotypical people might be. Typically, organizational tasks aren't the most stimulating, novel or interesting, so it's tricky for our brains to stay focused on these things.

- **Is often forgetful in daily activities.**
Working memory (more on this in **Chapter 1: Working memory, page 57**) is another of the executive functioning skills that are impacted in neurodivergent people, and so it's very easy for us to lose track of all the different things we need to do and remember each day. These differences in memory can mean that staying organized becomes much more tricky because we might forget what we need to organize in the first place.

- **Is often 'on the go', acting as if 'driven by a motor'.**
When you have a brain that feels as though it's whirring at a million miles an hour, thinking about a hundred things at once at any given time, it can be tricky to sit still long enough to organize those thoughts in any meaningful way, let alone organize the things around you or things you need to do.

Additionally, organization also requires us to have good time management skills, which is something that neurodivergent people can experience differences in. As I mentioned in **Chapter 5: Flexibility (page 202)**, ADHDers can experience something known as time blindness, which is defined as the inability to sense the passing of time and can show up in things like losing track of time, and underestimating or overestimating how much time has passed, how long a task will take, or how much time is left before an anticipated event. We tend to see time as 'now' or 'not now', and so organizing ourselves for future events or situations is difficult for us to conceptualize. Similarly, many other neurodivergent people can experience time in different ways. For example, studies have shown that people with schizophrenia have an internal clock that speeds up, slows down, and doesn't necessarily run at a constant speed, and people with bipolar or other mood disorders might notice a shift in how they experience time during manic episodes.

Which systems have affected the way we think about organization?

As with all the executive functioning skills that we have explored throughout the book, late-stage capitalism means that we place a disproportionate amount of value on someone's ability to stay organized. In a capitalist society, when we are working busy office jobs, perhaps juggling multiple jobs around childcare, housework, hobbies and socializing, there are lots of things to organize, structure, prepare for and keep track of at any given time. If productivity and money-making weren't such major priorities, we would not have so many documents to organize, projects to plan for and tasks to keep on top of.

Additionally, when consumerism is rife, we have more possessions in our homes, which means more and more things to organize and arrange. Research has shown that one in eleven American households rent a self-storage space which costs them over $1,000 a year in rent, and that home storage products have become a $4.36

billion industry. However, if we were to reduce the amount of 'stuff' that we owned, we would have fewer things to organize, meaning there would be much less strain on our executive functioning skill of organization – further research has suggested that getting rid of clutter eliminates 40% of housework in the average home. Add to this the fact that impulsive ADHDers, in particular, will be much more prone to buying things on a whim or being perceptible to marketing techniques, and we can see how we might suddenly have a whole excess of things to keep track of!

How can we support ourselves with organization?

I think that our ability to stay organized comes down to three main things, which are consistent with the themes that we have explored throughout the rest of the book. The first of these is letting go of the way that we've been told we 'should' organize things. If having things out on display (more on this in **Tip 3: Showroom chic, page 81**) works better for you than having things put away in boxes, that's fine. If you need to organize your thoughts visually or in a written format rather than keeping it all floating around in your head, that's okay too. If it makes more sense to organize your home by keeping different things in different rooms than would be expected, you guessed it, that's not a problem. As long as things feel organized, or helpful, to **you**, then it doesn't matter what they look like to anybody else.

Second, I think it's important to remember that it's okay for us to support ourselves by relying on help from the people or tools around us, whether that's needing a friend or family member to remind you about something, relying on a cleaner to help keep your home organized, or setting reminders about the things you need to stay on top of. You don't have to organize and manage every single thing by yourself all the time. The people, tools and services around you are there to help, so don't feel like you're failing by using them!

Finally, I think the last main way that we can support ourselves with organization is not to be afraid to make things as easy as possible for ourselves. It is much easier to stay organized if you have fewer things to organize (more on this in **Tip 39: Keep it simple, page 327**), and if you need to do things like colour-coding, labelling or keeping different boxes around your house to stay organized, there is no moral failing in that. There are no prizes for doing life in hard mode, and by letting go of some of the 'shoulds' we've had imposed on us, we can make life a whole lot easier for ourselves.

A list of things that are <u>absolutely fine</u>:

- Setting things up in a way that works for you, even if that isn't what you've previously been told is the 'right' or 'best' way.

- Relying on support from the people around you or automation to stay organized.

- Organizing things in a 'non-traditional way' if that way makes more sense for you.

- Not having your home or space 100% organized 100% of the time.

- Organizing and sharing information in a 'non-traditional way' if that way makes more sense to you, for example not having to always tell a story in a linear way.

- Relying on reminders and visual cues to keep yourself organized.

- Cutting down on the things you have, buy or commit to in order to have fewer things to keep on top of.

- Having to keep multiple different things in multiple places because you struggle with organizing yourself to remember them all the time – for example, keeping a spare phone charger in your car and at work so you don't have to remember to take one with you every day.

- Asking for all communication to come via a certain channel (e.g. only by email instead of email, WhatsApp, Slack and verbally) so that you don't have to keep on top of multiple sources of information.

Tip 36:
Homely hacks

By Sheri Smith (she/her) (better known as Forever Yours Betty), AuDHD content creator

We all know how important our surroundings are — especially when we are trying to navigate a world with AuDHD. In a life full of juxtapositions and extremes, it can be a challenge to create an organized space that works *with* your brain, but also brings joy! The true secret to creating a happy AuDHD home is knowing yourself, embracing your quirks, and not justifying your space for anyone but you.

1. Get to know yourself

First things first — you need to understand what makes you tick. One size does not fit all, so take some time to look at the parts of your life that you struggle with, and those that bring you calm. Things like your existing habits, attention span, and the stuff that helps (or hinders) your mood are important when creating a space that works for you.

For example, it's a common ADHD tip to suggest always having everything on show due to our object permanence (more on this in **Tip 3: Showroom chic, page 81**), but that isn't helpful for everyone! I find the kitchen to be the most overwhelming room in the house, and I thought having everything on show would lead to less waste and more cooking. However, I quickly realized that this was not for me. There were too many options, leading to decision paralysis. This is a stark contrast to my open-plan wardrobe, which gives me so much joy when I can see it all in front of me. I find the kitchen overwhelming, so seeing everything at once feels too much, whereas I find my wardrobe exciting, so seeing all my clothes at once is inspiring and a celebration to my eyes! **It's all about bridging the gap of your needs**.

2. Spot the hurdles

Identifying your weak spots is like finding a map to navigate your home better. Maybe clutter is your kryptonite, or lighting can throw you completely off track. **Take note, then take action!**

I struggle with clutter, but organizational piles have always been my friend. Solution? Everything that comes into my house needs to have a home – but since putting things back in their proper place isn't always feasible, I have a designated 'pile space' where things go while they are waiting to be put back in their home. This looks different in every room: a bucket in my wardrobe room for clothes that aren't dirty but need to be put away, some sticky hooks in the bedroom for hanging up clothes and towels instead of putting them on the floor, and a basket of miscellaneous bits in the bathroom.

3. Setting up for success

Now that you've got the lowdown on your needs, it's time to make your home a happier place for you to exist. Here are some tips I've gathered along the way that seem to work for most:

– Clutter control: Differentiate what you define as clutter. As a collector, I love seeing my favourite things around, but unwanted clutter is stressful. Have a storage solution in each room that can be used as a deliberate dumping ground to be organized at the end of the week. Insert this into your routine.

– Colourful cues: Don't be scared of using colour! Whether it's on your walls or creating a big bright calendar or colour-coded label, what would you do if you felt no one was judging you?

– Relentless reminders: I have a notepad next to my coffee machine for shopping lists, one next to my couch and bed for brain-dumping, and Post-it lists of what's in my kitchen cupboards!

4 Celebrate yourself!

You are not your challenges! If there's one thing about us, it's that we like what we like. Most of us have spent a large part of our lives diminishing the things that bring us joy, whether it was because people found it 'too much', or 'weird', or 'childish'. This is your chance to embrace ALL OF IT!

Dedicate spaces for your hyperfocus. Don't hide what makes you happy. It's YOUR space.

When I explained to the builder that I wanted twenty-seven kitchen cupboards made because I'd made twenty-seven various piles of what made sense in my head, I did so with my chest. For me, it makes most sense to have a place for breakfast food, food I can make in less than twenty minutes, and snacks, rather than separating them into dry or canned goods. This way, when I recognize the need, I have a cupboard that will help assist that need in a space I find joyful.

5. **Tweak as you go**

Your home is a living, breathing space that grows with you. Be open to change and know that what works today might need a little tweak tomorrow. Keep an eye on how you're feeling, and if something's not quite right, switch it up. You are bound to make some mistakes along the way; I know I have. But knowing what you don't want only means that you are one step closer to finding out what does work.

Turning your home into an ADHD and autism-friendly haven is all about **celebrating you**. With some self-love, homely hacks, and a dollop of your individuality, you can create a space where you feel not just at home, but **in your element**. So go ahead, dive in, and let your home be the comforting cocoon you deserve!

Tip 37:
Automate and delegate

As we explored in **Chapter 1: Working memory (page 57)**, our neurodivergent brains can struggle with juggling all the different bits and bobs that we are expected to. There are so many different things to remember and so many plates to spin at any given time that it's impossible for us to keep them all on track and keep ourselves organized. One way that we can stay organized while relieving some of the pressure that we're under is by working out which things we can **automate** and which things we can **delegate**.

Automate

If there are tasks that we need to do or things that we need to remember on a recurring or regular basis, there are different ways that we can automate these reminders so that it's one less thing to think about.

- I use a shaving **subscription service** so that I automatically get sent new razor blades every couple of months. Not only is this more sustainable, but it's just one less thing for me to have to consider. You can use similar subscription services for things like deodorant and toilet rolls, and Amazon even has a 'subscribe and save' option for a lot of groceries and toiletries. If you know you're going to need to buy new shower gel every month, why not automate the process so you never have to think about it?

- I **automate task reminders** in my Google Calendar app on my phone to remind me to order my repeat prescription and transfer my rent to my landlord every month. This means that I can just act when the reminder pops up, rather than spending the whole month thinking, 'I must remember to order my prescription before my tablets run out!'

- You can **automate regular payments and transfers** by setting them up as standing orders, direct debits or regular payments. Instead of having to manually transfer my rent every time I get the Google Calendar reminder, I could eliminate my need to do anything completely by setting this up as an automatic standing order payment that goes out on the same day each month.

- You can **use a home assistant** like Alexa, Google or Siri to automate reminders. When something pops into your head – for example, you order your repeat prescription after being notified by your automated reminder – you could say, 'Hey Google, remind me to pick up my prescription from the pharmacy in three days' time.'

- If you're wanting to save money for a certain something, you can **automate your savings** by using a tool like Plum, Monzo or Chase that automatically transfers money to a savings or investment account depending on certain rules you set. As an example, I use Plum, and it automatically moves money over into my investment account every week. There are all sorts of rules you can set up, such as rounding up the change from any money you spend, judging how much you're spending that week and calculating how much you can afford to invest, and even transferring a certain amount every time it rains in your area (a sure way to invest *plenty* if you're living in rainy Manchester like me!).

- If one of the areas you need more support with is in shopping, cooking for and feeding yourself, you could automate this by **using a meal subscription service** like HelloFresh, Gousto, Mindful Chef or any of the many others services out there. This could range from the delivery of ingredients and recipes being automated for you all the way through to some meal-prep services that will deliver ready-cooked meals to your door to take the entire process off your plate.

Delegate

If there are other tasks that we aren't able to automate but that don't specifically need our input and we know could be taken off our plate, we can delegate these tasks to somebody else – whether that be a service we pay for or a parent or carer, support worker, colleague, virtual assistant or friend. Obviously, this depends on the support you have access to, the people you have available around you, and your financial situation, and I know that I am in an incredibly privileged position to have access to as much support as I do. However, often there are things that all of us could take off our plate that we just never have because we've been told we have to be completely independent to be considered 'fully functioning' adults.

- When my LinkedIn account first started to really grow, I was still in full-time employment and so did not have the capacity to respond to all the messages and comments I was receiving every day. However, I knew that doing so would both be helpful to the people in the community I was building and help to grow my account even more in the long run. To help with this, I wrote a document of 'standardized' answers and replies to the most common questions and comments I received and then delegated the task of replying to my personal assistant, Luke (who helps me keep on top of various admin tasks and saves my life every day!).

- If you struggle to keep on top of all your housework (don't we all) and your budget permits, you could hire a cleaner to come to your house every couple of weeks or use a laundry service to pick up your dirty laundry and drop it off a few days later ready to go.

- A very simple and free example of delegation could be delegating the task of deciding what's for dinner each night to your partner, friend or housemate. Maybe the endless options send you into the pits of decision freeze and end up overwhelming you to the point that you don't eat anything at all; however, if someone else were to write a list of meals for the week, you might find it easier to just complete the instruction of preparing each meal on the day it was needed.

• My brother (who you heard from earlier in **Tip 18: Sampling sobriety (page 191)** can struggle to keep on top of the admin involved with ordering and collecting his prescriptions each month. Since he lives at home with my parents, he has delegated this responsibility to my mum, who orders and collects the prescription each month without him having to remember. It can feel uncomfortable to rely on our parents or partners to help us with things like this, but there is absolutely nothing wrong with having support needs and allowing the people who love us to support us with them! It could be a two-minute job for them which saves you endless hours of brain space and avoids crises if you don't manage to keep on top of it.

Essentially, what we're trying to do here is identify the things that need to be done for our lives to stay in good working order, but don't need to be done by us specifically. By automating and delegating these tasks and responsibilities, we're freeing up some brain space for the things that require our full attention, while making sure that we stay organized and on top of things. A win-win!

Tasks I could automate:

- _____
- _____
- _____
- _____
- _____
- _____
- _____
- _____

Tasks I could delegate:

- _____
- _____
- _____
- _____
- _____
- _____
- _____
- _____

Tip 38:
Time-blocking and monotasking

It's difficult to stay organized when you have a brain that loves to jump forwards and backwards between hundreds of different tasks at a time. We often feel as though we need to be multitasking and juggling lots of things all at once in order to feel (or seem) busy because we've been told that 'busy = productive'. In reality, though, this is often far from the truth.

Why do we think that running around like a headless chicken is the best way to be productive when, if we think back to the times that we've achieved our best or most meaningful work, I would guess that for most of us that would be during a time of focused, undistracted work? As an example, my best days of writing both this book and my first, *unmasked*, have always been when I've been on an aeroplane. This is because there was nothing to distract me from the one, singular task that I needed to get on with – I had no phone signal, no emails and no notifications to distract me. By contrast, if I try to write between meetings or when I have hundreds of email or WhatsApp notifications bothering me, it's unlikely that I'll get much done.

One way that we can work around this is by **time-blocking** our tasks together, and then **monotasking (a fancy way of saying doing one thing at a time!)**. When you are writing your to-do list, or doing your **Big Brain Dump** that we learned about in **Tip 26 (page 251)**, you first want to get all the tasks out of your head and on to paper.

Once you have done this, you can **group together similar tasks** and block out chunks of time to complete these similar tasks together. For example, if you have a whole bunch of admin quick ticks that you need to get through, you can block out a two-hour chunk in the morning to whiz through them. That way, you're able to get through all these quicker tasks that don't require deep concentration or focus at once, rather than trying to jump between deep work and quick ticks, which might leave you feeling frantic and all over the place.

Instead of your day looking like . . .

- 10 minutes of writing.

- Quickly reply to that email I needed to get back to.

- Work on the content concept that I needed to send over to the brand I'm working with.

- Another 10 minutes of writing.

- Reply to Instagram comments.

- Jump on a Zoom call for a virtual meeting.

- Another 10 minutes of writing.

- Get distracted by another email that comes through.

- Etc., etc.!

. . . you can whiz through the emails, comments and other admin quick ticks in a two-hour chunk in the morning, for example, leaving the afternoon freed up for you to really get stuck into the writing you need to do. Below, try to make a list of quick ticks that you could group together vs deep work that would be best monotasked.

Quick ticks	Deep work

Tip 39:
Keep it simple

This tip is another one that seems incredibly simple but can really make a big difference to the way that you're able to stay organized. It seems painfully obvious to say out loud (or type out!), but it took me a surprisingly long time to work out (!), so I'm sharing it in the hopes that it will help you, too.

It is much easier to stay organized if you have fewer things to organize.

That's it, that's the tip.

- It is much easier to keep on top of your laundry and have all your clothes neatly stored away if you have fewer clothes to wash, dry, iron, fold and put away.

- It is much easier to keep track of where things are in your space if you have fewer things to keep track of and fewer 'junk drawers/boxes' where you store all those random 'I might need it one day' cables, trinkets, instruction manuals and boxes.

- It is much easier to plan your schedule if you have fewer things to squeeze into it.

- It is also much easier to actually do all the things you need to get done if you have fewer things to get through.

Essentially, a minimalist lifestyle is much easier to keep on top of. If you have fewer things to lose, it's much less likely that you're going to lose them. If you have fewer things to remember, it's less likely that you'll forget them. If you have fewer things to keep track of, it's much more likely that you'll be able to keep track of them.

The fewer things you have to organize, the more organized you're likely to be. So why not try clearing things out by:

- Selling your clothes on Vinted or Depop (always price depending on the quality of the item so that you've got more chance of selling!).

- Selling things at a car boot sale (if you want to get rid, price things very cheaply!).

- Donating things to a charity shop (make sure to check what they will accept before you take them there).

- Taking anything that can't be donated to your local recycling point.

Tip 40:
Calendar comforts

In the same way that I recommended automating reminders in your calendar in **Tip 37: Automate and delegate (page 318)**, I'm going to take that one step further and recommend that you keep track of **EVERYTHING** in a calendar. And I mean everything.

I am personally a fan of a digital calendar, and use Google Calendar as my go-to, as I like to be able to move things around as and when they change and know that I'll always have it with me thanks to the handy iPhone app. However, if you're more of a paper person, you can use an old-school diary, too. The most important thing is that **every single thing** gets scheduled into that calendar.

So often, we think, 'Oh, I'll remember that!' or assume that if something isn't a meeting or appointment it doesn't need to go in our calendar, but that leaves us a) prone to forgetting things, and b) prone to overcommitting to things we don't actually have the capacity for because we don't realize how much stuff we actually need to squeeze into our days.

The only way that I'm able to stay organized in any sense is by completely and utterly living and dying by my Google Calendar. If something needs to happen, it needs to be scheduled into the calendar. That includes all the usual appointments and meetings that you'd expect to find, but also:

- Time blocked out for the work that I need to do that doesn't involve anybody else (whether that's the quick tick time blocks that we spoke about in **Tip 38: Time-blocking and monotasking (page 324)**, or a big chunk of time for **MUST WRITE BOOK**).

- One evening a week blocked out for housework, laundry and tidying.

- A fifteen-minute slot scheduled in to remind me to post any social media content that needs to go out.

- Chunks of time blocked out for my non-negotiables (more on this in **Tip 29: Prioritizing for YOU, page 258**) like reading, going for a walk or going to the gym (and even sometimes planning out when I'll have showers).

- Any travelling time blocked out (whether that's my drive to the studio, the time it will take me to get into town before an appointment, or train tickets and timings when I'm heading to London for work).

If something needs to happen, it needs to be in the calendar. Otherwise, it isn't happening. (A small disclaimer that I absolutely am not perfect at this and most definitely go through phases of being more and less disciplined with how much I'm scheduling in, but that life is *always* easier the more that goes into my calendar).

This not only helps me to stay organized and have everything that I need to remember all in one place (and in a place that happens to send me handy notifications ten minutes before the thing needs to happen), but it also helps me to see my *actual* capacity and so be more likely not to take too much on. In the past, I might have seen that I didn't have any meetings or appointments in my calendar for a certain day and assumed that meant I was free to make plans or say 'yes' to extra work, when, in reality, I needed to write, create content, eat, go to the gym, shower and catch up on my laundry. This can be a little bit tricky to balance with demand avoidance (more on this in **Tip 8: Avoiding demand avoidance, page 123**), but if you're using a digital calendar, you can always move the blocks around once they're scheduled in — what matters is that they're in there in the first place rather than floating around in your mind hoping that they'll be remembered.

Organization recap

Our final executive functioning skill, **organization**, is defined as the ability to structure and arrange information, materials or physical spaces. It essentially describes our ability to keep on top of everything and have it structured in a way that works for us. As my mum loves to remind me, 'There should be a place for everything, and everything should have its place!' Organization is the skill that allows us to feel as though everything is under control, and we know what is happening when, where to find the things that we need, and that there is an order to the things we are doing and our belongings.

In this chapter, we have explored:

- What organization is.

- The systems which have affected the way we think about organization.

- Some ways we can support ourselves with organization.

- 5 things to consider putting in place for your organization.

Your takeaway box

- There is not one correct way of being organized; to be organized is to have things arranged and structured in a way that works for you. Don't be afraid to do things a little differently in order to suit your brain!

- Our organizational capacities are more stretched than they've ever been before, since we tend to have so many more possessions to keep track of in our consumerist society and so many more tasks/appointments/demands on our time in a world that can feel like a capitalist rat race. If we can reduce the amount of things we have in our homes, it will be easier to organize the things we do have, and if we can say 'yes' to fewer things in our diary, then it will be much easier to organize our time. Less is more!

- When it comes to the things you can't get rid of completely, it might be helpful to rely on automation and delegation to support you in staying organized. If it is not completely necessary for something to be done specifically by you, then think about whether you can hand it off to another person, or automate it with technology.

Conclusion

When I first discovered that I was autistic and ADHD, I thought that unmasking was going to be a one-time, overnight, relatively simple thing: 'Aha! I know who I am now! I can be myself, and that's my unmasking done!' However, as time has gone on, I've realized that I couldn't have been more wrong. Even now, two years after my diagnoses, I'm probably masking the vast majority of the time. First, because it's a natural instinct that I jump into whenever I'm around other people, but also because of the sheer number of layers that there are to peel away.

I think I thought that unmasking would sort of be like peeling an orange: one simple layer to peel away, and then what was left underneath would be a whole, unmasked me. In reality, though, it's more like an onion: every time you peel back one layer, you find another hidden away – and sometimes, peeling them away can even end in tears.

And if we're running with the onion analogy, actually knowing what each of the layers are is a really tricky thing to do, because they're so deeply ingrained into the way we've been taught to live, function and behave – all the way from 'make eye contact' through to 'be able to deal with all of the demands of running a household by yourself'. We've often never questioned forcing ourselves through these things (even when they felt uncomfortable, or left us burned out beyond belief) – **because no one ever told us that we could question them.** Especially for those of us who grew up undiagnosed and unsupported, we'd never been identified as having anything 'different' about us (by doctors, parents or teachers – even if our peers could always sniff it out!), so we had no reason to question whether we had support needs, or needed to do things in different ways. We had to just put up with it, stick a smile on our face, and force ourselves to function in the same ways that everyone else did.

Often, we've spent such a long time forcing ourselves to function in this way that we completely lose sense of which parts of us are 'the mask' and which parts of us are *actually* us. As I explained in **unmasked**:

> Growing up as an undiagnosed neurodivergent person in a neurotypical world can mean spending a lifetime being gaslit, misunderstood and invalidated. Naturally, this can make us begin to question our own judgement or rely on validation from the world around us. If you have constantly been told that your sensory needs are invalid, that there's 'nothing wrong with you', and that you 'just need to get on with it like everybody else', you can imagine how you might start to lose that trust and confidence in your own ability to see things as they are.

On top of this, you've spent your whole life presenting as this person that wasn't *truly* you, often mimicking the people around you, so it can be really tricky to differentiate yourself from the 'character' that you've been playing. One of the most common questions I've received in my two-and-a-bit years of being a Person On The Internet is, 'How do I actually unmask?!' Often people discover that they're neurodivergent – whether that's through attaining a medical diagnosis or through self-diagnosing – and really **want** to start being more true to themselves and letting go of the mask that they've been wearing their whole lives, but they just don't know where to start. It can be such a daunting prospect for some that they actively choose to avoid unmasking and letting go of the things that make them feel safe. They know that unmasking will ease some of the psychological burden they've been carrying, and hopefully leave them feeling much happier and healthier and able to keep burnout at bay, but they simply don't know where to begin, or whether it is safe to do so.

In the past, I've found my answers to this question to be pretty insufficient or wishy-washy:

- **Be yourself!**

- **Do the things you enjoy!**

- **Trust that it will happen over time!**

Each answer *is* technically correct . . . but they are not incredibly helpful to a group of people who, by nature, need very clear, precise and specific instructions. They never felt very tangible, and I just didn't seem to be able to put my finger on what exactly it was that had allowed me to start dropping that mask and finding the glimmers of unmasked Ellie underneath. Through writing this book, though, and spending so much time thinking about all of the shoulds, woulds and coulds that society has imposed upon us, I've realized that, actually, **that** was the missing piece of the puzzle.

Unmasking, put simply, is saying goodbye to should, would and could.

If, every time you do something, you question, 'Am I doing this because it comes naturally to me, or am I doing this because somebody once told me I *should*?', you can start to identify the parts of you that are the mask, the layers of the onion that you want to peel back. If you find yourself answering, 'Because somebody once told me I should,' you can say goodbye to that 'should', and instead find a way of doing or being that feels more natural to you.

I *should* make eye contact – or, I **CAN** choose to look wherever feels most comfortable for me.

I *should* be able to remember everything on my own – or, I **CAN** ask for help when I need it or use different tools to make it more manageable.

I *should* be able to put on a brave face however I'm actually feeling – or, I **CAN** allow myself to feel my feelings, and turn to a friend to help me process what's going on.

I *should* juggle all the different household tasks on my own – or, I **CAN** ask for support from my housemates, or hire a cleaner.

I *should* be able to concentrate for eight hours at a time while sitting behind a desk – or, I **CAN** identify that I work better with regular breaks, movement and background stimulation.

And the list goes on, and on, and on.

As we've explored throughout the course of the book, there are an infinite number of these 'shoulds' that society has imposed upon us our entire lives that nobody has ever really stopped to question – 'That is the way it has always been done, so that is the way that we'll continue to do it!' In reality, though, a lot of it is . . . nonsense. Who decided that those were the best ways of doing things, and who were they to know what was *actually* best for each of us?

If we learn to let go of should, would and could, we can find better ways of doing things that better suit us as individuals, and, in the process, discover who we *really* are behind the mask.

And remember – there are no prizes for doing life in hard mode. One of the silliest 'shoulds' that I think society has created in recent years is this idea that the only path worth taking is the difficult one. We seem to have been tricked into believing that struggle, difficulty, and sheer hard work are some kind of rite of passage to being a 'good person' – and that anything we do to make things easier for ourselves is 'cheating' or 'lazy'.

'Hiring a cleaner is so lazy!' Or, maybe it's an incredibly smart decision for somebody who has identified that they don't have the time themselves!

'Using pre-cut veggies? What are you, a child?!' Nope, just an intelligent adult who has realized that food prep is a challenge and that she'll be getting the exact same amount of nutrients from her meal whether she chopped the carrots herself or not!

'Listening to an audiobook? That doesn't count as proper reading!' – Actually, it does! If you'd prefer to lie down in the dark and listen to your favourite story rather than strain your eyes and force yourself to concentrate, you'll still get the exact same ending!

Why is it that making life easier for ourselves is seen as cheating? The phrase 'an easy way out' is commonly used to imply that doing things the easy way is inherently not the best way, as though for our actions to have worth we have to expend extra energy. Shouldn't the point of life be to find ways of making it as easy, enjoyable and pleasant for ourselves as possible?

You don't have to force yourself through unnecessary struggles to have 'earned' the stamp of approval as a Good Person. You don't have to do things in a way that completely opposes your wants, needs and natural ways of being just because someone once told you that you 'should'.

Learning to say goodbye to should, would and could isn't only a great way of being able to achieve more while being a happier and healthier person; it is the ultimate act of self-love. It's a way of saying to yourself, 'I deserve to be happy. I deserve to be accommodated. I deserve to be **ME**.'

And we all deserve that.

Acknowledgements

I never thought I'd get the chance to write one lot of book acknow-ledgements, let alone two. So I want to start by saying an enormous thank you to **every single person** who has ever read, supported or interacted with my work for giving me the platform that has allowed me to do so many things that I'd never in my wildest dreams believed would be accessible to me.

Thank you to Amy for shaping *unmasked* into something I could feel so proud of, for taking the chance on me being a multi-book author, and for helping me to develop *how to be you* into the book it needed to be. Thank you to Rachel for truly hearing me and taking me from 'content creator with an idea' to 'multi-book Penguin Life author', and to Elise, Kayla, Sahina and the Penguin Life team for all your hard work in sharing *unmasked* with the world, so that they'd be open to reading book two, and for all your work on this book, too.

Mum, thank you so much for everything that you do. I can truly never say it enough. You're my rock, the only reason that anything has *any* chance of running smoothly, and the person I know is always on my side. Dad, thank you for all the time, patience and energy you've put into understanding and supporting me in really being 'me'. In the space of two years, I've seen you go from someone who found neurodivergence tricky to talk about, to someone who consistently accommodates me and advocates on my behalf. I know how much effort you've put into that, and it never goes unnoticed. Lewis, thank you for being my best friend. I'm so grateful for you every day and so proud of the unmasked person you're growing into. It brings me endless joy to see you sharing your funny, caring and enthusiastic self with the world.

Thank you to the entire Middleton and Pickering families for being my biggest cheerleaders – I really could not ask for a better family. Grandma Chris, for your supportive texts that always seem to come exactly as I need them, Grandad Jeff, for your kindness and calming influence, and Grandma Elise, for getting to grips with Instagram so you could keep up with what I'm up to and be my biggest fan.

Thank you to Alyx for always being there to listen to a tearful voice note or a frustrated rant, and to Scholes for making sure that no matter how much the world wants me to be Ellie Middleton, there is always space for ellie milburn. Thank you to Charli for being my same-brain twin and for your endless love and support, and to the whole hot + hilarious gang for showing me what a friendship group is supposed to feel like.

Thank you, Leanne, for always helping me figure things out, to Seran, Verity, Luke and Claire for being the organizational lifesavers and career-builders I've always needed, and to Evie for giving me the space and validation to empty out my thoughts every week.

And finally, thank you, **you**. For taking the time to read this book, for making it this far, and for loving yourself enough to know that you deserve to give yourself the kindness, compassion and consideration that you have always given to the people around you. Your bravery in accommodating and loving yourself is what gives me the courage to keep doing the same.

References and resources

Introduction

page 1 'My wonderful friend Leanne's book *ADHD An A to Z*'

Leanne Maskell, *ADHD An A to Z: Figuring it out step by step*, Jessica Kingsley Publishers, 2023

How to use this book and what to expect

page 14 'the mental processes that enable us to . . .'
https://developingchild.harvard.edu/science/key-concepts/executive-function

page 15 'first coined by Kassiane Asasumasu in 2000'
https://stimpunks.org/glossary/neurodivergent/

page 16 'approximately a 30% delay in the development of their executive functions'
https://ot4adhd.com/2022/08/01/

executive-functions-for-classroom-performance/

page 16 'approximately 75–80% of the executive functioning capability of their peers'
https://www.adhdaustralia.org.au/about-adhd/the-role-of-executive-functioning-in-adhd/

page 16 'up to 80% of those with autism suffer from executive function disorder'
https://www.leicspart.nhs.uk/autism-space/health-and-lifestyle/autism-and-executive-functioning-skills/

What defines our view of executive functioning?

page 23 'a racist ideology based upon the belief that White people . . .' Layla F. Saad, *Me and White Supremacy: How to Recognise Your Privilege, Combat Racism and Change the World*, Quercus Books, 2020

page 23 'White supremacy culture'

https://www.thc.texas.gov/public/upload/preserve/museums/files/White_Supremacy_Culture.pdf

page 35 'We need to recognize executive functioning as . . .' Sonny Jane Wise, *We're All Neurodiverse*, Jessica Kingsley Publishers, 2023

page 36 '*Why I'm No Longer Talking to White People about Race*'
Reni Eddo-Lodge, *Why I'm No Longer Talking to White People about Race*, Bloomsbury Publishing, 2017

page 36 *Dismantling Racism: A Workbook for Social Change Groups*
https://www.dismantlingracism.org/

page 36 'system of social structures and practices . . .'
https://ncca.ie/media/2601/sylvia-walby-v2.pdf

page 36 'women carry out around 60% more unpaid work'
https://www.bps.org.uk/research-digest/women-bear-brunt-unpaid-labour-and-it-may-be-affecting-their-mental-health

page 37 '80% of autistic women remain undiagnosed at the age of eighteen'
https://pubmed.ncbi.nlm.nih.gov/35204992/

page 37 'boys were diagnosed with autism at an average age of four years'
https://www.crossrivertherapy.com/autism/diagnosis-age

page 37 'studied eight boys and three girls'
https://www.ncbi.nlm.nih.gov/pmc/articles/PMC8531066/

page 37 'never met a girl with the fully-fledged picture of autism'
Uta Frith, *Autism and Asperger Syndrome*, Cambridge University Press, 1991

page 38 'patriarchy operates through six unique structures'
https://ncca.ie/media/2601/sylvia-walby-v2.pdf

page 39 'glass ceiling'
https://www.bbc.co.uk/news/world-42026266

page 40 '8.2% of CEO roles in large companies'
https://www.thecourieronline.co.uk/women-ceos-finally-outnumber-ceos-called-john/

page 41 'men do sixteen hours a week unpaid work . . .'
https://www.ons.gov.uk/employment andlabourmarket/peopleinwork/earningsandworkinghours/articles/womenshouldertheresponsibilityofun paidwork/2016-11-10

page 41 'relationship between increased housework and poor mental health in women'
https://www.bps.org.uk/research-digest/women-bear-brunt-unpaid-labour-and-it-may-be-affecting-their-mental-health

page 44 '52% of women believe that gender discrimination negatively impacts their medical care'
https://www.today.com/health/today-survey-finds-gender-discrimi nation-doctor-s-office-serious-issue-t153641

page 46 'an economic and political system'
https://dictionary.cambridge.org/dictionary/english/capitalism

page 48 'control by one power over a dependent area or people'
https://www.nationalgeographic.com/culture/article/colonialism

page 53 'Get your fucking ass up and work'
https://www.youtube.com/watch?v=XX2izzshRmI

page 54 'All Tangled Up in Autism and Chronic Illness'
Charli Clement, *All Tangled Up in Autism and Chronic Illness*, Jessica Kingsley Publishers, 2023

Chapter 1: Working memory

page 57 'My thoughts are stars I can't fathom into constellations'
John Green, *The Fault in Our Stars*, Penguin Books, 2012

page 61 'hold and manipulate information for short-term use'
https://childmind.org/article/what-is-working-memory/

page 61 'the magical number seven plus or minus two'
https://psychclassics.yorku.ca/Miller/

page 61 'young adults can recall only three or four longer verbal chunks'
https://www.ncbi.nlm.nih.gov/pmc/articles/PMC2610466/

page 62 'ADHD status was associated with very large magnitude impairments . . .'
https://www.ncbi.nlm.nih.gov/pmc/articles/PMC7483636

page 63 'not disabling if one has access to tools like a Dictaphone'
https://osf.io/cbk23/

page 71 'easier to remember a few small groups of numbers'
https://www.understood.org/en/articles/8-working-memory-boosters

page 75 '*Working Hard, Hardly Working*'
Grace Beverley, *Working Hard, Hardly Working: How to achieve more, stress less and feel fulfilled*, Penguin, 2021

page 78 'When teachers prepare to teach . . .'
https://pubmed.ncbi.nlm.nih.gov/24845756/

page 78 'people were taught about the Doppler effect'
https://www.nytimes.com/2019/04/12/smarter-living/how-to-improve-your-memory-even-if-you-cant-find-your-car-keys.html

page 79 'The best way to learn something truly is to teach it'
https://www.nytimes.com/2018/08/25/opinion/sunday/college-professors-experts-advice.html

Chapter 2: Self-monitoring

page 95 'the process of paying attention to our internal thoughts and processes'
https://www.foothillsacademy.org/community/articles/self-monitoring

page 97 'where an event occurs, but we [autistic people] don't process . . .'
Carly Jones MBE, *Safeguarding Autistic Girls*, Jessica Kingsley Publishers, 2021

page 101 'Masking may involve suppressing certain behaviours'
https://www.autism.org.uk/advice-and-guidance/professional-practice/autistic-masking

page 108 'We can't mimic others' behaviour unless . . .'
Dr Hannah Louise Belcher, *Taking Off the Mask*, Jessica Kingsley Publishers, 2022

page 113 'Emotion Sensation Feeling Wheel'
https://Emotion Sensation Feeling Wheel Handout by Lindsay Braman - LindsayBraman.com

page 131 'the extent to which someone monitors their self-presentations'
D. Day and D. Schleicher, 'Self-Monitoring', *Encyclopedia of Positive Psychology*, Vol. 19, Wiley, 2009

Chapter 3: Inhibition/impulse control

page 139 'the human brain uses a combination of hormones'
https://www.verywellmind.com/adhd-symptom-spotlight-impulsivity-5443083

page 140 'lower number of dopamine receptors in the brain'
https://www.ncbi.nlm.nih.gov/pmc/articles/PMC2958516/

page 140 'it triggers an even higher amount of dopamine'
https://www.science.org/doi/10.1126/science.1185778

page 141 'nine times more likely to end up in prison'
https://www.adhdfoundation.org.uk/

wp-content/uploads/2017/11/A-Lifetime-Lost-or-a-Lifetime-Saved-report.pdf

page 141 'far more likely than those without to engage in risky financial behaviour'
https://www.abc.net.au/news/2019-05-31/how-adhd-affects-your-wallet-mental-health-kids/11158952

page 141 '60% of ADHDers said that it directly impacts their financial lives'
https://monzo.com/blog/the-extra-costs-of-living-with-adhd

page 141 'four times more likely to have an eating disorder'

https://www.additudemag.com/
adhd-linked-to-eating-disorders/

page 142 'the act of walking leads to an
increase in creative thinking'
https://www.apa.org/pubs/journals/
releases/xlm-a0036577.pdf

page 158 'possible link to emotional
escalation'
https://pubmed.ncbi.nlm.nih.
gov/32898309/

page 164 'involves being able to control one's attention'
https://www.ncbi.nlm.nih.gov/pmc/
articles/PMC4084861/

Chapter 4: Emotional regulation

page 170 'the ability to exert control
over one's own emotional state'
https://www.psychologytoday.com/us/
basics/emotion-regulation

page 170 'having trouble steering your
moods'
https://my.clevelandclinic.org/health/
symptoms/25065-emotional-
dysregulation

page 171 'has been shown to uniquely
predict the following'
https://www.additudemag.com/
desr-adhd-emotional-regulation

page 173 'emotion regulation differences are prevalent in ADHD
throughout the lifespan'
https://ajp.psychiatryonline.org/doi/
full/10.1176/appi.ajp.2013.13070966

page 183 'it engages multiple senses,
requiring you to concentrate on the
present environment'
https://www.calm.com/blog/5-4-3-
2-1-a-simple-exercise-to-calm-
the-mind

page 186 'first coined by Dr William
Dodson in 2017'
https://metro.co.uk/2022/02/14/
what-is-rejection-sensitive-
dysphoria-and-how-to-cope-with-it-
16098492/

page 186 'this extreme emotional pain
is a result of the differences in brain
functioning'
https://www.psycom.net/adhd/
rejection-sensitive-dysphoria

page 194 'The Artist's Way'
Julia Cameron, The Artist's Way: A
Spiritual Path to Higher Creativity, Pan
Books, 1992

page 194 'The Art of Writing Fiction'
Andrew Cowan, The Art of Writing Fiction, Routledge Books, 2011

page 195 'I don't have anything else to
write about'
http://www.point-to-creativity.com/
automatic-writing.html

Chapter 5: Flexibility

page 216 'You'll see I wear only gray or blue suits . . .'
https://www.vanityfair.com/news/2012/10/michael-lewis-profile-barack-obama

page 229 'When we're asleep we want to stay asleep . . .'
https://speakingofautismcom.wordpress.com/2020/03/24/task-initiation-executive-functioning-and-autistic-inertia/

page 232 'Autistic brains process on average 42% more information at rest'
https://www.sciencedaily.com/releases/2014/01/140131130630.htm

page 234 'ability to switch between tasks and demands in response to changes'
https://lifeskillsadvocate.com/blog/executive-functioning-skills-101-flexibility/

Chapter 6: Planning and prioritization

page 254 'visual schedule could be a sequence of photographs'
https://ed-psych.utah.edu/school-psych/_resources/documents/grants/autism-training-grant/Visual-Schedules-Practical-Guide-for-Families.pdf

Chapter 7: Task initiation

page 272 'people with ADHD have at least one defective gene, the DRD2 gene'
https://www.ncbi.nlm.nih.gov/pmc/articles/PMC2626918/

page 275 'neuroemergent time'
https://www.martarose.com/freeresources

page 283 'four things that best motivate ADHDers'
https://www.tiimoapp.com/blog/adhd-task-initiation

page 300 'rewards trigger the pleasure centre in the brain '
https://www.hallowelltodaro.com/blog-raw-feed/2021/8/4/task-initiation-tips-and-tricks-for-getting-started

Chapter 8: Organization

page 307 'the average person loses up to nine items every day'
https://cdn.ymaws.com/www.napo.net/resource/resmgr/press_kit/press_kit_2020.pdf

page 309 'the inability to sense the passing of time'
https://www.verywellmind.com/causes-and-symptoms-of-time-blindness-in-adhd-5216523

page 310 'people with schizophrenia have an internal clock'
https://scanberlin.com/2019/12/15/time-perception-in-schizophrenia-do-schizophrenic-patients-perceive-time-differently/

page 310 'people with bipolar or other mood disorders might notice'
https://link.springer.com/article/10.1007/s11097-018-9564-0

Index